The Holiday Angler in Wales

First edition: December 1996

© Chris Thomas/Y Lolfa Cyf., 1996

ISBN: 0 86243 375 4

Photographs: Chris Thomas
Cover photograph:
A Welsh Mountain Stream, Cath Wheatley

Printed and published in Wales
by Y Lolfa Cyf., Talybont, Ceredigion SY24 5HE
e-mail ylolfa@netwales.co.uk
internet http://www.ylolfa.wales.com/
tel 01970 832 304
fax 832 782

The Holiday Angler
IN WALES

Chris Thomas

yl Lolfa

For Shirley,
with thanks for her patience.

Contents

SONNET TO WELSH WATERS

Due west of England's border one may find
A wealth of sparkling water, clear and bright,
Enough to please the fisher, any kind,
Whose soul is capable of sheer delight.
Wherever he may search to ply his art
'Mong savage crags or tranquil lakeside shore,
All things combine to levitate the heart
Encouraging contentment evermore.
From barren upland down through gorge and woods
And bee-buzzed meadows ere they reach the sea,
The waters touch the land with many moods
To soothe society's wounds, compassionately.
So, greetings, anglers, shed your harsh travails
In the bounty of the watery world of Wales.

Chris Thomas   1941-Not dead yet!

Preface

So you're thinking of taking a holiday in Wales and maybe doing a bit of fishing while you're there?

Well, why not? Just think of all the advantages! The natives speak and understand English – over 99% of them, in spite of certain misleading propaganda to the contrary. There are no worries about exchange rates. You can drive on the proper side of the road (as long as it is wide enough to boast at least two lanes) without additional insurance, international driving licence or strange motoring regulations to worry about.

There aren't any anti-Brit traffic cops or road tolls yet (except for a few bridges – and nobody forces you to use *those*; there are alternative routes). Drinking water is safe; so is bathing in the sea. Toilet arrangements are comfortably familiar and strange indigestible foods are rare unless a deliberate attempt is made to locate them, thus allowing delicate stomachs to remain stable and unabused. There are no worries about air traffic control or ferry strikes or leaks in the Chunnel.

Even the bugs are compatible thus eliminating the need for unpleasant jabs with their constant risk of nasty side effects. And if you cannot bear to be parted from the goldfish or the overpowering affection of your slavering hound you can either take them with you or put them into care close by without having to endure any tearful quarantine separation on your return.

In short, the advantages of holidaying almost on your own doorstep are manifold, combining benevolently to keep stress levels to a minimum. After all, that's why you go on holiday in the first place, isn't it?

Are there any disadvantages?

The answer to that is "very few" – and those which do exist are minor, usually very local in nature and of a type with which you should already be familiar. Things like heavy weekend traffic on the major holiday routes, parking in the larger towns and cities and maybe having to travel quite a distance when staying in the more remote mountainous areas if a sudden craving for a bag of fish and chips becomes uncontrollable.

"What about the weather?" you may cry. "It rains too much in Wales."

More rain does fall in Wales than in a large part of the UK, true, but most of it comes down in the winter. Summers, particularly in recent years, can be just as sunny and hot as many foreign destinations. Wales is no more immune to the so-called "greenhouse effect" than any other part of the world though there is much less chance of contracting malignant skin cancer. Medical treatment is free, too.

In fact, the rain is one of Wales's many great blessings. Not only do several large English cities depend upon water piped from the Welsh reservoirs but a goodly supply of the wet stuff is necessary to maintain a high water table in the mountains and keep the rivers flowing.

The fact you are reading this little book at all means you

have an interest in all sorts of water, 'cos that's where the fish are, and you, being a dedicated fisherman, intend taking a relaxing holiday getting to grips with some of them. Furthermore, there is no good reason why an angling holiday should be restricted to the summer months. Brown trout and migratory fish are out of bounds in the winter, of course, but many lakes are available to cast for rainbow trout; grayling still have to make a living out of the occasional fly and there are plenty of rewarding venues at which to do battle with coarse and sea species. Accommodation can be much cheaper in winter, too.

This kind of thing is what the author has been doing for many, many years. Not only on holidays but weekends, odd days off and any other spare time not taken up by important chores (and there are not many of those which can't be left until another day). All the major rivers in Wales have captured his dry and wet flies in the clawed branches of their predatory waterside trees, his worm hooks among their seemingly carnivorous rocks and his spinners in their inaccessible and immovable underwater snags at one time or another. Most of the tributaries, large and small, he has sampled, with rents in clothing and scratches on tender flesh exposed to bramble and thorn to prove it. Many of the upland brooks he has explored with varying degrees of success.

It is not only game fish which wake screaming with nightmares at his approach (or more likely laugh themselves sick at his fumbling efforts). He has stalked coarse fish in the picturesque lakes, ponds and canals – at times with only chilblains and the initial signs of frostbite to show for his labours.

He has pursued with vigour a large variety of sea fish from the wave-booming rocks and surf-sided sandy seashores. What could be more natural for him but to attempt to advise visiting fishermen of the ins and outs of Welsh angling in order that they may enjoy their holiday to the fullest and hopefully come back for more of the same.

Besides which, the Welsh economy needs the money!

Some might point to the fact that much of the text could equally have been written about the fishing prospects in any other mountainous area of the British Isles. Take away the place names and the rest would be just as relevant.

There is truth in this. But Wales is a very special place – ask any Welshman – and there is no part of Britain which has such a variety of good fishing in such a small area.

It is taken for granted you are already a reasonably proficient angler so there will be as little as possible in the way of trying to teach you to suck eggs. At the same time it is realised many visiting anglers may be unfamiliar with the character of most of the rivers close to where they will be staying and may fill the car with tackle they probably won't need. A raging Welsh torrent or high mountain tarn requires different equipment and treatment to your average placidly-flowing English river.

The down-side of paring tackle to the absolute basic minimum is that there are few things worse than losing a good fish for lack of a landing net, for instance, even though experience dictates you have never needed it before where you are fishing, and anyway, you probably wouldn't have hooked the fish in the first place if you'd brought it along. Such are the mysterious workings of fate. Still, any experienced angler should be well versed in the practice of finding something to blame for a bad day.

Each sort of running water and each type of fishing will be taken in turn, followed by practical and pragmatic advice, warts and all, on how to minimise disappointments, wasted time or an irritating day out. If a few toes are trodden on, a few feathers ruffled or even shrieks of dissenting rage induced at some of the observations in these pages, well, most of the facts can be verified and maybe the airing of them will encourage rectification of some of the more irritating turn-offs encountered by holiday anglers who may vote with their waders and spend their vacation elsewhere the following year. It is to be hoped such observations are taken in the spirit with which they are written; that of sincere and hopefully constructive criticism which may go some little way towards improving the environment, the facilities and the attitudes met with at Welsh watersides. And the rest of the UK as well, come to that!

Rules of engagement will be suggested and recommended areas for the best results in divers angling disciplines will be prescribed. A few anecdotes are included as examples of what Welsh waters are capable of producing (with a little good fortune) – only one of which contains a realignment of the exact truth. One has to protect the innocent and consider one's self-image, after all. Careful consideration of all the relevant points to watch should ensure you get the best out of your holiday.

Now read on!

Welsh Rivers

(Their characters and what lurketh therein)

IT IS SAID there are over 15,000 miles (24,000 kms) of river in Wales. Yes, someone has actually taken the trouble to measure them. In actual fact, this must be considered a conservative estimate as the unknown compiler of this figure gives no indication of how small a watercourse has to be before it is disqualified from inclusion.

The two longest rivers are not strictly Welsh although most of their courses are in Wales and both have their sources high in the Welsh mountains. These are the Wye and the Dee (or Gwy and Dyfrdwy, to give their correct titles) which are 130 and 111 miles (209 and 179 kms) long respectively. The longest British river, the Severn at 220 miles (354 kms) in length, only has its upper reaches and head-waters within Welsh borders.

There are three totally Welsh rivers over 60 miles (96 kilometres) long; the Usk – 85 miles (137 kms), the Teifi – 73 miles (117 kms) and the Towy – 68 miles (109 kms). Many are over 25 miles (40 kms) long including a few tributaries of the major rivers. A lot of fishable running water by anybody's standards.

So where shall we start? There are so many rivers in Wales. Most are well worth fishing; from tiny, treeless mountain brooks

The upland brook which produced 19 fish (Chapter 1) is in this picture. No, not the one on the right – it is the barely-seen trickle, left of centre, coming from the stone wall.

with their small, hardy trout, through roaring white-spumed chasms and gorges to stately, meandering flood plains where muscular salmon and sea-trout glide athletically upstream. All have their virtues and disadvantages. They can be roughly divided into three groups if one takes the approximate width of the river as a measure. Each of these groups has its own characteristics and individual method of approach. They are the high mountain waters, upper, middle and lower reaches and they will be discussed in turn. Let us begin with a general picture of the upland brooks.

Major Welsh Rivers

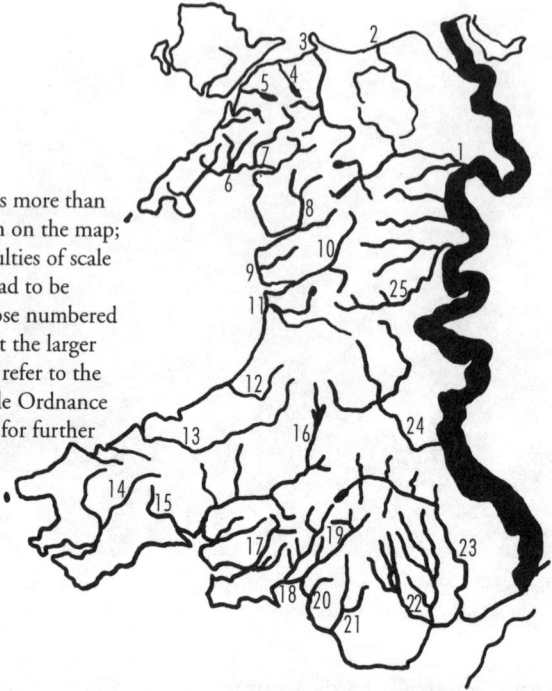

There are lots more than can be shown on the map; due to difficulties of scale many have had to be omitted. Those numbered below are just the larger rivers. Please refer to the 1:50,000 scale Ordnance Survey maps for further guidance and detail.

1. Dee *(Dyfrdwy)*
2. Clwyd
3. Conway *(Conwy)*
4. Ogwen
5. Seiont
6. Dwyfach/Dwyfawr Complex
7. Glaslyn
8. Mawddach
9. Dysynni
10. Dovey *(Dyfi)*
11. Rheidol/Ystwyth Complex
12. Aeron
13. Teify *(Teifi)*
14. Eastern & Western Cleddau
15. Taf
16. Towy *(Tywi)*
17. Loughor *(Llwchwr)*
18. Tawe
19. Neath *(Nedd)*
20. Afan
21. Ogmore/Ewenny Complex
22. Taff & Valleys Complex
23. Usk *(Wysg)*
24. Wye *(Gwy)*
25. Severn *(Hafren)*

Chapter 1

The High Mountain Waters

The fountain's fall, the river's flow,
The woody valleys, warm and low,
The windy summit, wild and high,
Roughly rushing on the sky.

John Dyer   1699-1757

IT IS ALWAYS a good idea to purchase an Ordnance Survey map
(1 : 50,000 series) of the area where you intend to stay when
on holiday. Even a cursory glance at it will reveal an enormous
network of thin blue lines branching and dividing like the veins
in the ear of a white rabbit or a cabbage leaf held up to the
light. They are more noticeable in the high mountains and
moorland regions where there are fewer roads and other things
to clutter the map. These thin blue lines indicate the course of
a river; the thinner the line, the smaller the river. The very
thinnest ones running across the high contour levels are those
we are interested in at the moment, the ones in and on the
mountains.

Wales has a lot of mountains, this being the principal reason
so many delight in holidaying here – and the rumour that they
block out the view is an outrageous lie! More than 60% of the

country is over 500 ft (152.4 metres) above sea level – a good thing to remember when global warming really starts to take off. There are 168 summits over 2,000 ft (609.6 metres) including 15 over 3,000 ft (914.4 metres) – all of the latter being in Gwynedd.

Although they are all privately owned, these mountains can be climbed, walked upon, camped on or fished by Joe and Jane Public and those others who just want to escape the over-regulated, cut and thrust maelstrom of modern society. To the commercial interests within that same society the mountains have only one reason for their existence – to be utilised for profit regardless of any other consideration.

Forestry interests, for instance, have a lot to answer for, although it must be admitted they may have seen the error of their ways and now appear to be making a genuine attempt to take a more sensitive approach. Whether this public-spirited attitude will survive increasing privatization is open to speculation. Walkers and anglers beware!

None the less, large areas of mountain are covered with fast-growing conifers, and more plantations are planned together with their access roads gouged into the slopes. The latter, winding in twisting alpine hairpins up the steep valley sides, together with hundreds of acres of drainage ditches and grids, remove water as fast as possible with no regard for what this is doing to the water table. Maybe the angler could live with this if it were not for the fact that pine forests concentrate acid from the atmosphere in the streams, their shade destroys other forms of life both on land and underwater, and angling is often actively discouraged within their borders.

A new threat to the accessibility of upland regions is looming on the horizon – literally. Subsidized wind farms, often funded by foreign interests who couldn't care less about the Welsh countryside, are proliferating. This activity will bring yet more access roads torn from untouched slopes, more interference with drainage patterns, and their own grid of ditches to reduce the water table still further. Walkers and anglers pottering around the high pastures will be viewed with suspicion by security-conscious officials and it will take only one act of overt sabotage to ensure that these subsidized windmills sitting in their subsidized moorlands will be surrounded by subsidized fences to keep the dangerous public out altogether.

Nevertheless there are still an enormous number of untouched areas left; quite enough to accommodate the robust walkers and anglers who visit them every day. Nearly all the tops of these mountains are pretty well devoid of trees and, as a result of this, the small streams in the uplands are completely open to the blistering heat of summer, the dismal gloom of low pressure areas, and the harsh, frozen clamp of winter.

These tiny dribbles of water come in a number of forms. There are some which just peaceably trundle along through the bracken, heather and peat, and are usually found on the very tops of the mountains where the lie of the land is often relatively flat. Further downhill they increase in speed as the slope steepens. It is within this section that the glacial inheritance of Wales shows its intrusion. Deep, scooped valleys radiate outwards from the great rocky massifs and most of the upland brooks will fall into one of these at some time in their plunge towards the lower lands. Depending on the steepness of the valley sides and the character of the underlying rocks, the brook may either cascade down in a series of cataracts, brawl between rounded boulders clad in lichen and moss, or simply tip over the edge as a waterfall. On reaching the bottom of the valley there is often a more tranquil stretch before the main watercourse is reached.

It would take either a brave or a very stupid trout to attempt to run up some of these brooks; more likely very stupid as it can be jolly hard to make a living up on the "Tops". None the less, it is surprising how they manage to get up some of them, particularly those with waterfalls. Some are very high indeed and you would think no fish could possibly jump over them, and indeed many can't. Nevertheless large numbers of trout are to be found above some of these waterfalls. They are never stocked. How they got there is a source of wonder and a variety of conflicting theories.

More and heavier rain falls on these uplands compared to the lower-lying areas; over 100 inches (254 cm) per annum in places, while the average for the rest of Wales is about 40 inches (101.6 cm). This is a perfect meteorological situation in which to erect huge dams across narrow sections of the steep-sided valleys to contain the flow of water and pipe it down to the towns and cities.

Rain here can sometimes be of monsoon intensity, flattening grass, bracken and heather with the sheer volume of airborne water. Winds, much stronger at high altitudes, can lift water from the surface of the tiny pools, blow cataracts sideways and spread this flow of spray many metres from the stream. Sheets of clear water flow swiftly downhill among the tough, sheep-nibbled mountain grasses; only a few centimetres deep, maybe, but many metres wide and travelling like a greased pig on roller skates in its rush to reach the most convenient brook and out of those inhospitable surroundings.

Mountain brooks hasten bank high at such times. Upland vales shout with the music of rushing water, dark with the stain of peat, foaming in the waterfall pools like best bitter straight out of the tap. Dangerous places, these, in heavy weather; not to be taken for granted. Easy enough to break a leg on the wet rocks or in a hole in the ground where the waters rush unseen. Take care!

Where there is rain there are clouds and these clouds often glower low enough to obscure the top, even the whole of the mountain. Fishing in an upland brook at such times has to be seen in the same way as an expedition into a strange land. Go properly equipped, draw a rough map and put it in a see-through freezer food bag to keep it dry. Tell someone the area you intend to fish, when you expect to return, and watch out for the clouds getting lower and thicker.

Even for someone accustomed to the mountain mist it can be rather surreal. Sounds are muffled, sight can be restricted to a poorly-defined circle of just a few metres. There is no horizon so it is difficult to tell how steep a slope may be until you start to slide. A flatulent sheep tearing mouthfuls of bitter grass from the sward just outside your range of vision can invoke a primeval feeling of sheer terror if you make a habit of watching films in the genre of *Jurassic Park*. If ever you are caught out in the mist never try to take a short cut back to the road. Always follow the brook back down the way you came, keeping it in sight, or at least earshot, until safety is reached, and make sure you start back well before it begins to get dark.

In some cases there may be a road following an upland river valley using it as a pass (or *bwlch*) to get from one side of a mountain range to the other, but most of the mountain brooks either pass under the roads on their way to the main water course or are at some distance from any easy vehicular access. The holiday fisherman will have to be very fit or enthusiastic to get to these, which is one reason they can often be so surprisingly bountiful.

The former mining valleys in the south-east abound with brooks like these. Usually spring-fed at some point up the valley side, they clatter down past rows of old miners' houses, along the back gardens and through culverts under roads and footpaths. Often used as playgrounds by the local children, some of these streams will hold quite a fair head of fish, the main disadvantages being the urban surroundings and the attentions of friendly locals.

The aquatic life present in Welsh mountain brooks can range from zero to abundance. There seems to be no fixed pattern; two brooks in adjoining valleys carved out of the same type of bed-rock and with identical flora can be at opposite ends of the scale. Those having their source in, and issuing forth from pine forests, it must be said, are invariably sterile. The only sure way to find out if there are any fish in a particular brook is to have a go. If there is no sign of success after a quarter of an hour or so then the brook you have chosen is either affected by unnatural acidity or it has a habit of drying up completely during times of low rainfall. Even so, certain pointers can minimize the chances of wasted time.

The recent phenomenon of acid rain leaves its mark on the bed of a stream and in its water. Crystal-clear water is usually a bad sign – neat sulphuric acid is crystal-clear too – especially when it is accompanied by clean stones and a lack of water plants or algae. Looking under a few water-immersed stones will reveal no sign of insect life, and where there are no insects there are very rarely any trout. Even so, the autumnal urge to migrate upstream for spawning is a powerful one and trout can often be found in these unhealthy waters after a prolonged spell of heavy rain. They don't survive for long, neither do any of the eggs they may disperse.

So strong is this migratory instinct that the author has discovered fish in roadside gutters and mountain drainage ditches which only contain water in heavy rain and remain dry at all other times. At the very headwaters of some mountain brooks where there is only a series of unconnected, narrow pools in a shallow valley among the heather or bracken, trout can be found after rain. These adventurous pioneers don't last very long either, of course. When the rain stops and the channels dry out animals and birds quickly dispose of the pitiful remains.

Just as in other areas of the UK, all mountain land in Wales belongs to somebody. The difficulty is often finding out who owns the bit you wish to fish, but a visit to the nearest pub or farmhouse can often provide this information. Always try to obtain permission from the owner! Sometimes a fee may be asked for, but not always, since high mountain brooks are rarely considered worth fishing. This is not always the case, however. Some, indeed many, can give excellent sport.

The ones to look for are those which have insect life under

the stones and plenty of variety in the local flora on the banks and under the water. The flanks of the Brecon Beacons have large numbers of these, as do the Arennig and Rhinog ranges north of Bala and Dolgellau and the massif almost surrounding Blaenau Ffestiniog – indeed most mountain ranges can boast a great number of inhabited waters. Small brook trout abound in these tiny trickles, those showing the typical discolouration of natural peat often being the most prolific. Fish up to half a pound (227 grams) are not rare and many are to be found within only a few hundred metres of where the brook develops its permanent flow.

Most of the high mountain brooks are nearly impossible to fish with a fly because they are so small, and even a short cast can bridge the length of several pools. Spinning is out of the question: any brook big enough to use a spinner ceases to be high mountain water by definition. Worm or live insect is the only practical method. Use a size 6 or 8 hook threaded with a worm just big enough to cover all the metal with about a couple of centimetres dangling.

You may land more fish with a smaller hook but the trouble with this is the chances of the poor creature completely swallowing the hook are increased. This often entails a butchering job or even total disembowelment to retrieve the hook, and the remains of the unfortunate fish are unlikely to survive when returned to the water. No weights are needed unless the wind is so strong that the placing of the bait is uncontrollable. Even so, the trick is to get as close as possible to the little pools, unknown to the fish, if only to ensure that your bait is actually landing in the water and not resting on the bank to the dismay of any hungry trout which may be watching.

High in the hills with a fly. Dennis, the experienced angler seen here, caught some nice mountain trout on this day.

Stealth and concealment are very necessary attributes when fishing the small highland waters of Wales. Many are flanked with short grasses but no bushes, let alone any trees. Concealing yourself can be very difficult under such circumstances. Use what cover there is. Crawl (or roll along) on your belly if necessary. It takes very little in the matter of motion or the heavy fall of a careless foot to startle the dark little trout. Under the nearest stone they'll flash, instantly, and the opportunity is lost. Some brooks are so steep though, it can be very easy to hide yourself as the pool you are fishing could well be above your head.

Travel light! That's the secret of a good day's sport with small brook trout. Fish that are fat and big enough to look good in the frying pan are not very common, so you will not have to carry a creel, bag or net. Waders are rarely necessary, a pair of comfortable rubber knee-boots is all you require. Just take your rod, reel, hooks, thin nylon for traces, a few shot in case the wind gets up and your bait, comfortably unaware of its probable future, in a small jar or tin. Wear clothing in keeping with the weather forecast and put your few items of tackle in the pockets – not forgetting to include your rod licence. Feed and water your body before starting out. That's it! It can be tough enough fishing in rugged terrain without having to lug a load of unnecessary tackle with you.

For those who have nothing but contempt for highland brook fishing there is little to be said, except to advise them to remain in their overfished and artificially stocked big rivers and leave the brooks alone for the real enthusiasts. For those others who prefer solitude and the chance of an exciting day's sport a little anecdote of a fishing trip 'way up in the hills' may be of interest.

Early July, somewhere in the Brecon Beacons, and it hadn't rained for weeks. The water table was still high, though, and an acceptable flow of water could be seen through the binoculars. The car was parked up out of the way of other traffic and a coin was flipped to decide who was to have which brook. Then came the slog in suffocating, windless heat over the mountain to the venue.

On arrival just below the junction of the two brooks tackle was prepared for action. The two fishermen then split up; one to each brook. One was the main watercourse, flowing in a shallow valley over rocky ledges and under the occasional tree, withered and stunted by the harsh environment at this altitude. The other brook was a very small tributary just following the slope of the mountain. No valley contained it, hardly even a depression in the ground; just a thin split in the peat; a barely-seen line through the heather. We shall follow the angler fishing this one.

The first pool produced no response. It was too shallow anyway; nowhere more than five centimetres deep. The next, about a metre long and thirty centimetres wide, contained a hungry trout. There was a definite take but the fish escaped. A fish was caught in the next pool and admired before being returned to its tiny home. Almost completely black it was, wild as any mountain fighter with bright red spots, few but brilliant. From then on the pace became fast and furious. Worms went to their doom inside gaping, ravenous mouths at an alarming rate. Some of the pools were almost completely hidden by the heather, while others ran under the peat itself and could only be fished from above – down the hole where the water vanished. The trout cooperated with the fisherman for all they were worth. Nowhere was the brook more than a metre wide but often it was much more than that in depth and who knows how far the hidden pools extended sideways under the thick heather and peat? Many held several fish.

It took about an hour and a half to fish all the tiny pools up to where the brook began. It just issued abruptly out of the base of a drystone wall. The ground the other side of the wall was a marshy strip thronged with tough marsh grass and with no clear watercourse; simply a substantial spring welling up at a weak point where overlying limestone rested on a less porous rock. One moment there was the tinkle and plash of running water, the next – nothing. The end of the stretch had been reached; a full hundred and fifty metres from the place it joined the main watercourse.

About forty pools were fished in that short stretch. The total catch was nineteen trout ranging from 4 to 10 inches (10 to 25 cm) in length, all of which were returned to the water unharmed, but undoubtedly in a state of shock at having been discovered in what they thought was going to be a safe and undisturbed haven. At least as many more fell to the allure of the delectable worms but escaped. The fisherman went back to the car and waited. Two cigarettes later the other fisherman returned, devoid of worms and reported a total catch of fifteen fish of similar size range.

Such an outing, although somewhat better than usual, is not exceptional, so let nobody convince you there is no sport to be had in what appears to be an insignificant trickle of mountain run-off. What the fish lack in size can often be exceeded greatly in compensation value by their sheer numbers. Those who avoid such places are bereft of meaningful appreciation by definition and cannot consider themselves "compleat anglers", due to their lack of comprehensive experience.

Not all tiny brooks are on top of a mountain. All the lower valleys have small rills wandering through cultivated, as well as pasture lands, or straightened to serve as drainage ditches alongside the hedgerows. Travel between any two Welsh towns and you will cross over dozens of them, many of which you will not even see. Some are shrouded by dense undergrowth; passing under the road by means of a narrow pipe. Others may merit the construction of a proper bridge. These lowland brooks can be every bit as good and sometimes much better in the matter of results obtained, although they are generally very difficult to fish owing to the greater amount of plant life. Don't forget these! Some hold remarkably large trout.

So try a couple of high (or low) Welsh brooks on at least one day of your holiday. As long as there are enough pools more than 25 centimetres deep, and it is obvious that the brook never dries up completely, you could be in for a very pleasant surprise.

Chapter 2

The Upper Reaches

Dear stream! dear bank, where often I
Have sat and pleased my pensive eye. . .

Henry Vaughan   1621-95

SMALL UPLAND TRICKLES following the mountain slopes downhill
are joined by others in quick succession until a more substantial
body of water is created flowing in a properly defined valley.
The point at which an upland brook becomes the upper reaches
of a river is open to debate. For the purpose of this discussion it
will be assumed to be from the highest point a migratory fish is
likely to reach in a rainy year (where the stream is about 3
metres in width) down to where salmon and sea trout always
manage to get (about 7 metres wide).

The character of these streams can vary just as much as the
upland brooks. Some, for instance, will remain on a steep
gradient, such as the Ceiriog near Llangollen or the Rheidol
and Ystwyth which reach the Irish Sea at Aberystwyth. Others
in relatively more level surroundings ease their rate of descent
to a marked degree. Examples of the latter would be the Teifi at
Strata Florida abbey or the Arrow, west of Hay-on-Wye.

In north Wales there is yet a third type commonly found among the rugged crags and chasms of Snowdonia. During the great Ice Ages there were a great many active and fast-moving glaciers in this region due to the higher ground and the steepness of the original slopes. As a result, a large number of basins scooped from the underlying rock and moraines, built from the debris by the bulldozer effect of glacier snouts, were left when the ice retreated. Lakes were produced in both cases. Most of those in the permanent basins are still there (Glaslyn, Crafnant and Llyn y Gadair), as are many which formed behind the moraines (Llyn Padarn, Nantlle and Gwynant).

In a large number of cases, however, the outwash of rock, silt and dust carried down from the melting ice simply filled up the most shallow of these lakes, spreading out to level the bottoms. At the same time the lake overflow at the moraine dam end was slowly cutting away at the unconsolidated detritus, thereby lowering the water level. Eventually a balance was reached and the lake bed became a marshy wetland. The river, in spate, now carried most of its burden of silt right through the marsh and out the other end but a little remained after each flood. Grasses, bushes and trees grew in this rich loam enabling a lot more silt to be retained. The ground became firmer, the stream channel more permanent, until the old lake bed hardened into the feature we see today, a flat area through which the stream twists and turns forming deep pools on the bends and long placid canals in the straight bits.

In heavy spate conditions the streams in these stretches can still overrun the banks and deposit a little more silt, but this is generally balanced by the erosive processes at work on the banks as the river-bends gradually migrate downstream and across the valley. It is a microcosm of a flood plain. These sections of the river can be a delight to fish as long as there is not too much riverbank tree growth; a perfect example is to be seen on the River Ogwen upstream of Bethesda in Nant Ffrancon Pass, alongside the A5 trunk road.

Between these two extremes of slope can be found streams of all other types, either open to the weather or lined with a virtually impenetrable cover of trees and bushes, where the only way to fish is to wade up the centre and assume the stealth of a heron.

Typical upper reaches water in Cwm Nantcol; a beautiful stream but not easy to fish.

In just about all waters of this width the fishing is of superlative quality if trout are your main quarry. They are among the last of the places it is possible to find naturally wild fish in relatively undisturbed surroundings. A few streams, mostly in the southern ex-mining valleys, have been artificially straightened to minimize erosion to the banks, particularly where coal tips used to stand. Now flattened and landscaped to avoid a repetition of the ghastly disaster at Aberfan, the tips are still there; they've just had their shapes changed, now cover a lot more ground, and are prettied-up. Where they abut onto a water course they can erode with dismaying speed in spate conditions and create dangerously steep, crumbly banks, unless preventative measures are taken. Typical illustrations of this are to be found on the Lower Clydach river in the Swansea Valley and in the Cynon Valley at Aberdare.

Streams on many other rivers tend to fall into gorges during this part of their course. Most of the south Wales rivers like the Tawe, Towy (*Tywi*), Neath (*Nedd*) and many others do this. Getting down to the water can often be difficult and sometimes dangerous, but the rewards can be considerable in terms of the spectacular surroundings as well as the quality of the fishing.

Smallish trout abound together with a vast number of salmon and sea-trout parr. The tributaries of the Usk (*Wysg*), Wye (*Gwy*) and Teifi are especially prolific although most of these are private water and, as always, permission to fish should be obtained before venturing on to their banks. There are very few ticket waters on such streams throughout the whole of Wales, with the exception of those included with some of the major associations as part of their overall holdings. If there is a river of this size near where you are staying, that you particularly want to fish, approach the nearest farm and ask. A little negotiation, sometimes accompanied by the payment of a small fee (a couple of fish for the farmer and his family is not uncommon) will often readily achieve your objective.

Of course there are a lot of streams of this size which are not tributaries or headwaters of larger rivers but flow directly into the sea at this stage. Examples are the Afon Llan and Afon Lliw complex to the west of Swansea, the Dulais east of Colwyn Bay and the Desach south of Caernarfon. Small though they are, sea-trout and the occasional salmon find their way into them from summer onwards and share the limited supply of water space with the indigenous trout. Though hard to stalk and catch successfully, except in flood time, it is a memorable achievement when they are.

Fishing these adolescent streams can be a task best suited to the most skilled of anglers. They are, however, excellent training grounds for getting to know how to fish properly. Mostly small pools, big enough for a fly but rarely enough room to work a spinner, tangled undergrowth, slippery bare rock or cluttered boulders, it is often not easy. Yet if your taste runs to plenty of action with a chance of catching a fairly large fish in good condition (in some streams the fish are remarkably big for the amount of water available), these are the places to try. Food supply is usually good and huge hatches of fly can appear at times.

If your holiday ticket includes a stream of this size, set aside at least part of a day to have a go and find out the truth of the enthusiastic acclamations above for yourself. Bear in mind that it may be an off day for the fish as it can be in any other place, but, assuming all is as it should be, you can increase your chances of getting good results as follows.

It is always a good idea to have a look at your prospective venue before deciding which method to use and commencing to fish. The lie of the land and the accessibility of the water may mean an alternative approach to your preferred procedure. Unless the stream is heavily overgrown, meaning that you will have to do a lot of wading, or in spate, it is usually not necessary to wear waders. A stout pair of Wellington boots will be quite adequate and this can be a boon on a hot summer's day. Many of these streams will share their valley with some sort of lane or track, so parking the car must be done with consideration for others wishing to pass. Don't block farm or field gates unless you wish to be asked to vacate the premises immediately.

There is a tendency for many more bridges to be built over small streams to provide access to farms and tributary valleys. A parking place of sorts can often be found close to these bridges, gradually enlarged over the years by the vehicles of tourists and other anglers. Some of them are very old, rustic works of art in their own right with their masonry arches and holes at the sides to allow the passage of storm-spate levels. Camera enthusiasts can enlarge their albums to good effect with snaps of these picturesque and mostly unknown Welsh bridges.

A landing net is an unnecessary encumbrance but it is useful to carry a creel (or Tesco bag in the poacher's pocket) in case a couple of fish big enough to complement the chips waiting back home are caught. Please do not remove more from the river than you need for a nice meal; you may wish to return another day.

Dry or wet fly can be deadly if there is sufficient space to wield a rod. Use a short rod, as short as you like, with appropriate line and a short tapered nylon cast on the end of the line no longer than the length of the rod and half as much again. A longer cast will be almost impossible to control with any accuracy – and accuracy is all-important owing to the size of the pools. The flies can be of almost any variety; fish in the upper reaches are not very choosy. Anything remotely edible-looking will be attacked with gusto. In fact, these waters are a good place to use up the flies you normally wouldn't bother with on the larger rivers and this will leave your stock of favourites for more sophisticated quarry in the bigger waters and lakes on other days of your holiday.

Keep as far away from where you are casting to as possible. If you have to get close, use stealth and the greatest caution you are capable of. When wading move slowly and deliberately; it doesn't take much to startle fish in such close proximity. Always work your way upstream; it will rarely be possible to approach the water any other way without fish scattering in all directions.

Spinning can sometimes be used on the more open waters but the average pool can be fully explored in just a few casts, none of which entail more than a couple of turns of the reel handle. Movement upstream is likely to be rapid, frustrating and unrewarding. It is not normally to be recommended.

As in the high mountain waters the ubiquitous worm is the most suitable bait. In low or normal levels put on a somewhat bigger hook, about size 8, with just enough worm to cover the metal and leaving a bit of tail dangling invitingly. Use no weights if you can help it, but if forced to do so use the smallest shot you can get away with to cast the required distance without too much of a splash. The reel should carry all-nylon line about 6lb (2.72 kg) breaking strain with a short leader of 3lbs (1.36 kg). Keep your head down, slither through the grass and bushes to the pool, on hands and knees if necessary, and cast upstream to the likely spots. If you have to stand up in plain view of the water to land a fish (or retrieve the hook from a bush) you may just as well go on to the next pool. All signs of fish will have disappeared from the one you have just disturbed.

In high or spate water the next size up hook should be used and a bigger worm (or bit of one). Brandlings will still do the job but are more difficult to thread on to a bigger hook and tougher for a hungry trout to locate in a muddy, rushing stream. Medium to large garden lobs will do the trick nicely. Think of the mechanics of what happens to loose items beneath the surface of swirling, fast-moving water in spate and the reasons should become clear. Heavier shot will be required to ensure the bait sinks rapidly and stays down where it is needed.

If all goes as it should, an exciting day of pitched battle 'twixt angler and quarry should ensue. It can be pretty tiring too, all that creeping up the stream bent double and stretching up to the clawed branches of thoughtfully located trees to retrieve your tackle. It's worth it though, as a little anecdote of an admittedly exceptional day, not very long ago, will illustrate.

Close to the edge of the Denbigh Moors it was, just below the tree line. Heavy rain had fallen two days before, but not since, and the stream chosen had almost returned back to its average level. There was a little space to tuck the car out of the way by the stone-arched bridge leading to the farm. Less than

50 yards (45.7 metres) away the main road thundered with unceasing Saturday tourist traffic. This noise was to remain with the two fishermen throughout their session because the road ran parallel to the stream the whole of the stretch.

A light westerly wind hardly stirred the water and there were enough clouds to dapple the mid-August landscape. Very pretty! Upstream of the bridge there were very few trees, just occasional isolated willows shading some of the pools. In the second meadow upstream a large herd of evil-looking black cows – with horns, yet – grazed placidly with a scattering of calves. A careful study through the binoculars revealed no bull among the larger animals, just the usual protuberances associated with the female of the species. A mutual decision was made to run the gauntlet. Downstream, tallish oaks and willows lined both banks.

Several fish were perceived tucking into a late lunch and the use of a dry fly was decided upon. One angler set up a blue dun with an extra white hackle added to compensate for ageing eyesight. The other angler chose a Coachman because of its floating abilities and the fact the stream showed a strong peaty stain. Both walked downstream well away from the water and began fishing in their normal manner. Been fishing together very many years, these two, so the one who fished the first pool last trip stood by while the other cast the first fly. Straightaway he caught one fish and lost a couple more. The other angler fished the next pool and caught two fish while his colleague watched. Thing were looking good!

Fishing alternate pools as was their custom, several fish were caught by the time they had worked back up to the bridge.

Above this point the terrain altered abruptly and there was much more room in which to manoeuvre. The pace increased as the two anglers worked slowly upstream. No matter where the fly ended up, there always seemed to be a fish available to attack it. In small pockets at the sides of even the fastest runs, peat-stained trout with yellowish sides lunged from their lairs to give chase, often missing the fly because of the speed at which it was travelling.

By the time the second meadow was reached the intimidating herd of cows had wandered indifferently into another meadow away from the stream. The waterside activity continued unabated. The Coachman was lost in a large fish to the usual accompaniment of gnashing dentures and foul language. Its replacement proved just as deadly. Trout flopped on to the banks and were returned to the water with monotonous regularity. It started to get boring.

At the beginning of the last meadow before the tiny village it was decided to take a rest. A clear space was located among the cow pats and layers of sheep droppings and the two tired fishermen slumbered in the afternoon sun. Later, refreshed and adorned with blotches donated both by the fierce orb in the sky and the local insect life, a resumption was made about two hours before dusk. The fishing, if anything, was livelier than before as hordes of flies hovering over the water performed their evening procreative rituals of self-sacrifice.

It was agreed to keep two fish apiece as long as they weighed more than three quarters of a pound (340 grams). This was achieved within half an hour and included a beauty of nearly a pound and three quarters (794 grams) taken in the pool above the village bridge along with another of a pound and a half (680 grams). A gaggle of tourists watching from the parapet viewed the proceedings with noisy encouragement.

An attractive pool below the old road bridge over Afon Glaslyn at Nant Gwynant.

Until the time when it became too dark to see the fly on the water the quality of fishing diminished not one whit. From the final pool about 400 yards (365.8 metres) above the village bridge it seemed an unending walk on sore feet back to the car but no complaint was passed. It would have been churlish and ungrateful in the extreme. Trout could still be heard splashing about in the darkness now the traffic had almost ceased. A tally of results – the Blue Dun had caught 62 fish and the Coachman 53. When one remembers that for each fish landed another three were missed the enormous number of fish in this little stream is put into perspective – and it had never been stocked!

The Blue Dun used that day now rests in the author's drawer of reminders of memorable days; not much left except a shred of mole fur and a wisp of chewed hackle but the fish seemed to like it well enough even in that state. The stream? Well it still provides superlative fishing although not quite so frenetic as on that particular day.

Much of the most spectacular scenery in Wales surrounds these upper reaches and they are generally the cleanest and most unspoiled. Many have the remains of old mine workings, some dating back to pre-Roman days, and the later ruins of associated buildings crumbling into the ferns and heather.

Such remains endow the upland valleys with an atmosphere of history and introspection, slumbering away the dreams of "the good old days" with their short life expectancy, starvation and harsh social order. Long may they stay relatively untouched by agricultural expediency.

To descend into an upland valley on a calm, sunny day in mid-June with the sweetness of rowan and late hawthorn flowers scenting the air can be nothing short of a joy. The stream can be heard chuckling below, invisible under a dense canopy of trees. It may look impossible to fish, yet once beneath the trees down in the sun-dappled glades and dells beside the water there is often more than enough room to cast a fly with a little care. Such surroundings make life worth living. The harshness of the world seems a long way away.

Enough of that! In a nutshell, the holiday angler will find little to complain about in the headwaters of Welsh rivers. Most of the time they are sparkling clear and, with the exception of occasional interruptions by ramblers, it can be very peaceful. Even these interruptions are rare because most hikers tend to follow the footpaths (as they should) and there are not too many of these actually running alongside the streams; they tend to be some distance away. A further blessing is that these streams are too small for canoes.

Further downstream, however, in the middle reaches, such intrusions become more obvious as there is enough water to float on and the valley floors are subject to greater use by campers, walkers and others wishing to exploit the use of the rivers. It is this section we shall deal with next.

Chapter 3

The Middle Reaches

Where the pools are bright and deep.
Where the grey trout lies asleep.
Up the river and over the lea,
That's the place for Billy and me.

James Hogg   1770-1835

As a small stream flows down a valley between high mountain slopes it is joined at intervals by others, some of a similar size, until at last it contains sufficient water flow to allow it to be called a proper river about twenty feet (6.1 metres) or so in width. Downstream from here, unless it shortly falls into the sea, it can properly be called the middle reaches of an average Welsh river. Migratory fish can be found in these waters from quite early in the year so don't forget to take tackle suitable for them, as well as for brown trout, on your holiday.

In Wales the gradient of the valley usually begins to level off at this point, but there are many exceptions, particularly around the Snowdonia massif in north Wales. Because the high ground is so close to the sea in this area, most of the debris dumped when the ancient glaciers melted extends from the base of the precipitous upland slopes right down to the beaches. As a result, rivers outward bound from the mountain passes have to pick their way through ground consisting of smooth, rounded boulders embedded in a stiff clay.

This glacial boulder-clay fills the bottom of the valleys between humped shoulders of solid bedrock which radiate from the central highlands, gradually disappearing underground. The rivers continue towards the sea following the general slope of the country through courses running between large, mossy boulders randomly jumbled in an obviously geologically recent trough in the ground. Just have a look at the Llyfni, the Seiont, Ogwen and Gwyrfai tumbling and swirling in their beds, if examples are required. Proper pools are few, long stretches of fast white water common. This does not detract from their effectiveness as fisheries in the slightest. Indeed, it may enhance them because, with the exception of the rare pools and certain sections meandering across the beds of ancient, silt-filled lakes, virtually any little bit of still water behind a rock or near tree roots can hold one or more fish.

It can take quite a time to fish one of these boulder-filled rivers properly because there is an enormous number of possible places for a fish to hide, many more than on rivers in the south and west which generally contain far more pools. This is not to say the rivers there are inferior in any way – just different, and therefore they require a different approach when fishing them. Success in rivers of either type depends upon the ability to read the water correctly from above and fishing accordingly. For the sake of newcomers to angling in Wales here are a few hints.

Let's take the types of middle reaches found in the majority of Welsh rivers first. Mostly these will be found to be bigger versions of the upper reaches described in the preceding chapter but with an enhanced water flow. The average size of trout tends to be larger than upstream owing to the better food supply, although there may be more competition for what is available from the parr and fry of migratory fish, many of which supplement the diet of the larger native trout.

On some rivers such as the Teifi, the reduced gradient allows a verdant growth of water plants. Indeed, the Teifi is the nearest thing to a real chalk stream found in Wales and some very large

Clear, sparkling and small, but prolific in the right conditions.
Afon Dysynni at Pont Ystumanner.

trout stalk the deeper pools engendering fear in, and removing an occasional chunk from, their smaller brethren.

Dry and wet fly, spinner and live bait, in fact anything permitted by the owners of the water can be used to good effect. Waders are essential because the river may have to be crossed several times if full benefit is to be obtained without making too many tiring diversions up and down steep banks. A bag for the catch is also worth carrying: many of these rivers are stocked by angling clubs with keepable fish and a trout can get very grubby and gritty if carried in the pocket as well as becoming partially mummified on a hot day.

Stealth is less important, an asset to the lazy, the elderly or the infirm, but this does not mean the fish are less easily scared. Just take care to be as quiet as possible, keep out of the quarry's "window", and all should be well.

In the rougher north-western rivers dry fly is a bit difficult to use except in low water conditions or in the ancient lake-bed stretches. There is simply a shortage of calm bits of water on which to float a fly long enough to allow a trout to react and grab it. A sunken fly with or without droppers is much more practical in most places so a supply of these should be included in your holiday kit.

Spinning is quite feasible but bear in mind the number of snags to be found in a boulder-strewn river and the vast amount of weed thriving in the quieter stretches. Be prepared to lose a few expensive spoons or Devon minnows until you become accustomed to your chosen river and fish *all* the water, even the shallow parts. Migratory fish, especially, can be found in the most unexpected locations in rivers of this character.

As for the reliable worm, a little more can be added. Use at least a size 6 hook to allow for the survival of smaller fish – everyone knows trout have a mouth any mother-in-law would be proud of. In low water use shot as small as you can get away with and get as close to your potential prey as possible. In high water, of course, enough weight must be put on to get the bait down to the fish before it is swept away. On these boulder-strewn rivers don't just fish the larger pockets of water; every little lie downstream of a rock could hold a very large fish – even a salmon. Explore these small niches thoroughly and with care and you may be pleasantly surprised.

There is one form of fishing which can be extremely rewarding in the middle reaches of Welsh rivers (and elsewhere, no doubt). This is the art of fishing for sea-trout and even salmon with a dry fly.

Hang on, though! Surely the taking of a floating fly is evidence of a deliberate feeding pattern and quite distinct from the snatch at a spinner, wet fly or worm which is said to be a reaction to irritation or memories of familiar sea life. Sea-trout and salmon don't feed in fresh water, do they?

Yes, they do. Not all of them; most stick to a diet of fresh water and live off their fat until they return to the sea. A certain proportion, however, see no reason why they should suffer excruciating pangs of hunger simply because it's not the done thing. Autopsies performed on the river bank will show about 10% to 20% of sea-trout will have some form of fresh water life in their digestive tracts, mostly surface flies and larvae and often small fish such as minnows. The drier the weather and the lower the water throughout their time in the river, the more likely it is such remains will be found.

It follows that sea-trout, and sometimes salmon, *do* occasionally succumb to the temptation of a small, easily-captured snack. But certain conditions have to be in place.

The first is that the fish should have been in the river long enough – which means sufficiently far upstream from the sea or during a long spell of low water conditions – to develop a good appetite. The second is that the main run of sea-trout must be present in the stretch in which you wish to try your luck, and this means late in the season – from mid-July onwards at the earliest. Lastly, the river must be low because the fish are then more likely to stay in the same pool for a while.

In low water there is also a greater concentration of fish per cubic metre of water and dry fly fishing is easier in these conditions anyway. River fish always rise more freely at such times and there is more likely to be a reasonable hatch of fly on the water.

If all, or at least most, of these conditions are fulfilled, the discerning angler may consider that a try at dry fly fishing for migratory species is worthwhile. After all, trout can also be lured at the same time, can't they?

Particular attention should be paid to the location and behaviour of rising fish. Trout tend to take up position where they can obtain food with the minimum expenditure of energy – at the side of the current or in almost static water. It is worth remembering more energy is required to ride high in the water than to stay close to the bottom. Trout attempt to stay in the best place they can defend until they are ousted by a more aggressive fish, succumb to the lure of annual congress, are washed downstream, or get caught. These fast-food outlets are highly prized among trout and bitter disputes for their possession often take place between the more permanent inhabitants of the pool. Any change from this general rule, for example a rise in a location you would not expect a trout to lie, should be viewed as a possibility for catching a sea-trout on a dry fly.

A sea-trout normally displaces a greater amount of water than a trout. It follows that a voluminous breaking of the surface will indicate the presence of either a big brown trout or a migratory fish. Naturally, either would be acceptable to the average angler. The rises made by a particular fish, however, may be totally unlike the regular bobbing made by a brownie – several rises may be made in the space of less than a minute then there will be a gap of several minutes before another flurry of activity comes on. The chances are now greater that you are dealing with a sea-trout.

The feeding activity of your fish may also be in a location where either very small fish usually huddle out of the way of their larger brethren, or smack-bang in the middle of water fast enough to discourage the most energetic brownie. Shallow or deep, it doesn't seem to matter, although a favourite position is in the slower-moving and often shallow area found at the side of the main current at the head of a pool away from the main water flow. It is now almost certain your quarry is a sea-trout.

One further characteristic remains, and this is the most important of all for identification purposes. The rises will occur over an area of up to 100 square metres. When this is seen you either have a big shoal of large brown trout rising in turn in a place where they are not normally found or you have one or two sea-trout roaming the area. This is the way sea-trout behave when surface feeding. Their active natures will not allow them to remain in the same spot for long and it is the most reliable way to identify them from their rises alone.

All you have to do now is catch your fish. Use a bigger fly than you would for brown trout, size 12 or preferably 10 with plenty of hackle, bigger if you like. A sea-trout has a very large, soft mouth and is rather more difficult to hook securely than a brownie. Pattern is not as important as colour. It must at least look like a fly and be in natural shades: bright or fluorescent materials can rarely tempt a surface-feeding sea-trout during daylight hours.

Having tied on the fly, where do you cast it? The horrible truth is that it is simply a matter of chance. A sea-trout, being of a restless and energetic disposition, will roam over quite a large area when surface feeding and is just as likely to be heading towards you in his searches as away from you.

You will have to fish as if you were on a lake. Watch for a while; "case" his movements and try to ascertain the limits of his patch until you think you know where he will be heading next, then cast. This lessens the chances of being wrong and unless you are really clumsy you should be able to have quite a few casts at him until he recognises the danger signs. Surface-feeding sea-trout, for some unknown reason, are nowhere near as wary as when they are lying idle or travelling upstream. Perhaps this activity takes extra concentration on a small area of the surface and the wider field of vision diminishes in importance. Just don't make a noise, try to be inconspicuous and your reward will eventually come – often rapidly followed by stomach-knotting despair when a big fish with a big mouth proves to be too much for your little fly to hold on to. On the other hand. . .

Any holiday angler would do well to consider fishing for sea-trout during the hours of darkness. This is indisputably the best time to take a fish on a sunken fly as well as extending the time you can spend on the water, but be sure you are familiar with the contours and hazards of the river before you try it! And don't fish alone! At least for the first few outings.

Without lapsing into a lecture about how to achieve success at night, one point is worth mentioning. Most of those who tell you it is not worth going out when the moon is bright are talking through their collective hats. Firstly, it's a lot easier and safer for someone not familiar with the river to get around. Secondly, it is easier to spot where the fish are showing and cast to them without snarling up your line on every little bit of twig within fifty metres of the water. And thirdly, it's the perfect time to tie a big, bushy fly onto your top dropper.

When the moon is bright, sea-trout are inclined to fall for a dry fly more often than at any other time, They seem, at least to the author, to keep to the deep water and come close to the surface on bright nights. It's also surprising how often you meet up with those who advised you against it.

Try it and see. But no matter how bright the moon, never forget to take a torch with you.

So many anecdotes spring to mind to describe how excellent the fishing can be in the middle reaches of the average Welsh river it is difficult to choose one. Perhaps the following will

A fine salmon-holding pool right in the middle of a former south Wales coal-mining village with a road on either side. There are several more just out of sight upstream on this reasonably-priced ticket water.

give a suitably ambiguous picture.

It certainly turned out to be a full day on a local river! It was early in the season with flurries of wet snow interspersed with periods of intense and brilliant sunshine. Three trips were made out that day. The first one, starting at first light, didn't last long. An experienced angler had agreed to show a novice friend how to use a worm in average water conditions. After a hair-raising descent over thirty metres down a near-cliff to the river running fast through the gorge, the angler kept up a running commentary to the novice of what he was doing, and why, whilst removing and returning six fat, recently-stocked trout from the first pool. The novice, suitably impressed, and not realising such an initial catch was as much a surprise to his mentor as to himself, wobbled in his shiny new waders over the sharp, slippery ridges of rock to the next pool fifty metres upstream.

His first cast was unsuccessful, landing on the bank. Ignoring, or more probably unable to hear the bellowed exhortations of his tutor over the roar of the river, he moved closer and stretched further to cast.

The splash as he landed in the icy water scattered any fish which may have had his number on them. Instantly he was gripped by the current. Up in the air went the waders as his shocked face disappeared beneath the foam. Normally a good swimmer, he was utterly helpless as his back bounced along the bare-rock bottom, kept there by his waders retaining their air and acting as floats. Two podgy green legs sticking straight up in the air plunged rapidly downstream like a large and mildewed inflated rubber wishbone. A wildly waving hand broke the surface just before the deep water of the pool below could claim him for ever. More by luck than design it touched, then seized, a strong tree root hanging from the wet, rocky cliff on the other side of the current. It held. A dripping figure hauled itself snorting and shivering from the water, still holding the rod in a death-grip.

With much ado, blistering language, and the aid of a dead branch located in the strip of debris at high flood mark, he was helped to safety. It began to snow; large, wet flakes like bits of a cold, used poultice. The victim had turned a dreary shade of puce by the time they both got back to the car but warmth from the heater on the way home helped to ensure nothing worse happened to him other than a snivelling cold for the next week.

The experienced angler returned to the same place and continued. It was mid-morning by now. Eight nice fish were caught, two kept, then everything went quiet. No matter how invitingly the worm was presented in the most likely spots, the fish simply didn't want to know; an experience familiar to any fisherman. He returned home, had his dinner (fresh trout, butter beans and a few chips) then took an afternoon nap to compensate for getting up in the middle of the night to go fishing.

On reawakening, a bit of digging in the garden helped to avoid possible wifely criticism as well as providing the opportunity to capture enough worms for the following day. The weather became slightly warmer, the snow clouds disappeared, and the last couple of hours of daylight were set aside for a return to the river. The stretch immediately below that fished in the morning was elected owing to its less turbulent nature. A good hatch of springtime flies was often seen here hovering over the long, shallow pools and rippling, mossy runs.

In weather conditions totally unlike those of the early morning, the angler commenced his hopeful labours. Sure enough, plenty of flies danced over the water in the clear spring sunlight slanting through the leafless trees lining the banks. A March Brown wet fly was tied on the point with a dry Medium Olive pattern on a dropper about a metre above. There was hardly any wind.

Fishing downstream, two tiny fish were caught in the run at the head of the first pool but nothing in the main body of the pool despite the large numbers of rising fish. Both took the March Brown. A long, wide and shallow ripple extended down to the next pool and this was tried in spite of the fact very few had ever been taken here before. This time seven fish were landed, all undersized. With the anticipation of better results in the next pool it was fished very carefully and thoroughly. Fish bounced about all over the place – many flies were settling on the water now that the sun was low in the sky – but not a single one took any notice of the artificial ones temptingly displayed in their midst.

The same frustrating events occurred in the third and last pool to be tried. Only one fish, definitely over a kilogram in weight, felt sufficiently suicidal to actually hang on to the fly for a hop, skip and jump across the surface until reason returned and the tasteless shred of fur and feathers was spat out with obvious contempt. The angler stuck to his guns with increasing exhaustion until well after it became dark, without any success. Finally he packed up and stumbled back to the road, listening to the trout still splashing madly behind him.

Later that evening, the implications of what could have been the outcome of the early morning expedition came home to him and he resolved to be a lot more careful in future. He couldn't swim, you see. He still can't, and consequently has since treated all rivers with the respect they warrant when fishing alone. Make sure you do the same! It's not just a matter of getting wet. It is quite possible, even easy, to drown.

A further lesson to be learned is that it can be difficult to achieve a good catch even when the fish are hyperactive. Accept this as part of the mystery in the workings of the piscine brain – more obscure than that of the human female (and that's saying something!). Be glad the fish are still there and enjoy your failure, as far as you can, otherwise you may become depressed and lose confidence in your ability to fool fish. Angling is a sport, not a set of targets to be achieved. Leave that kind of behaviour to the so-called "managers" of this world.

Only a week later, in highly unpromising conditions, the last stretch described above produced a fine catch of eleven trout ranging from half a pound (227 grams) to over a pound and a half (680 grams) in weight. Not a single small fish showed its mouth above the surface.

Just goes to show, doesn't it?

Chapter 4

The Lower Reaches

We sought the riverside, elate, to try
The salmon catches with a new-made fly.
In Pwll-y-Gwaidd, perchance – oh happy luck!
A rushing plunge! The kingly fish has struck!
Sullenly to the bottom down he sailed;
There nosing, showed his brightsides, silver-scaled.

Richard Hall   1817-66

FOR THE FINAL description of our tour around the Welsh rivers we shall examine the lower reaches. As mentioned before, this designation should rightfully be employed even when the river enters the sea straight out of a boulder-filled gully, as can be seen on the Ogwen near Bangor or the Artro south of Harlech. However, the most common picture of the final stages of a river is that of a slow-flowing, stately body of water, secure in its own strength and permanence, winding over a flat-floored valley though a series of long, slow pools tipping from one to the other over shallow, rippling runs.

Every section of Wales has at least one example of this type. The Wye and most of the other southern rivers end their journeys through such environs. Moving up the west coast there are the Teifi, Ystwyth, Dovey and several others. On the north-facing coast there is a significant difference in character until the Conway, Clwyd and Dee are reached. By then the mountains have been left behind and the muddy banks and beds of the English rivers take over.

This is the main difference of the Welsh rivers compared to those over most of England, south of the Pennines at least. The typical lower reaches are mostly gravelly and, due to the storm-spate nature of Welsh rivers, have very few stretches flat and calm enough to allow mud to accumulate before the sea estuary is reached. The water flows clear and sparkling most of the time, except when the level is very low in drought conditions. During such periods the multi-coloured pebbles become covered with slimy, dark green algae, bits of which are continually breaking away to drift downstream looking for hooks and artificial flies to foul with their unpleasant embrace. Fishing can be very difficult then; only the use of a floating fly can avoid the worst of the algae. Fortuitously, low water is the best time to fish dry fly, anyway. Fast runs become accessible at these times.

In contrast, spate conditions produce a different hazard. How often have you heard flood warnings transmitted on the radio with special reference to the Dovey, Conway and Towy? Quite often, no doubt. Other rivers also spread beyond their banks – the Tawe, Neath, Loughor, in fact most of those flowing in flat-floored valleys with a low rate of descent to the sea are prone to spreading far afield after long periods of heavy rain. All have to be treated with the greatest respect and caution at such times. Preferably they should be avoided altogether and an evening in the pub contemplated as a somewhat inferior

"As the sun sinks slowly ... etc." A fine loop on the Dovey at sunset – the best time to start fishing for sea trout.

substitute. It is frighteningly easy to find yourself marooned on a bit of high bank unless a close watch is kept on your escape route.

When a river is as high as this, fishing is pretty much a waste of time anyway. Few rivers fish well on rising water or in fully coloured spate conditions. The best thing to do is try one of the tributaries if you don't really want to stay at home all day. Some rivers can rise to a full flood in a remarkably short space of time as years of relentless land-drainage works, open-cast mining and afforestation take their revenge. Rain no sooner falls on the land than it almost immediately finds itself in a ditch designed to get rid of it into the nearest river and thence out to sea as quickly as possible. Instead of soaking gradually into the water table, most of it runs off more rapidly than nature intended, thundering violently in spate down to the lower reaches.

The worst part of it is the inability of artificially drained land to sustain the water flow for any useful length of time and allow it to enter the rivers in a naturally controlled manner. Consequently the river level drops as rapidly as it rises. One quite large south Wales river regularly goes from low water to high spate and back to low water again in less than a day. It is as well to be aware of these rapidly changing conditions. A river too high to approach safely in the morning could be quite all right to fish with a dry fly by the evening.

There is one notable exception to this general state of affairs. The noble Teifi! Near the top of the middle reaches is a huge natural sponge called Tregaron Bog (or more properly, *Cors Caron*). Periods of heavy rain after a dry spell are stored in this porous, peaty material, and for a long distance downstream only the tributaries swell the main river. After the rain stops this stored head of water perculates slowly into the river and can keep the water level up quite high for several days. When surrounding rivers are back to low water the Teifi will still be running bank-high, clear and fast, just like a chalk stream. The trout have been known to throw caution to the wind at such times and migratory fish to take the opportunity to travel.

Most of these lower reaches have at least one club or association managing the fishing so obtaining a day or weekly ticket should be relatively easy. This will be discussed in chapter eight. For now, the quality of the fishing will be brought into focus.

Put briefly, it is nearly always of excellent standard. Trout of good size abound due to the restocking efforts of the clubs. Migratory fish move upstream from very early in the year, the best runs occurring from about July onwards. This accords nicely with the time most people are thinking of taking their holidays and game fishermen considering coming to Wales should bear this in mind.

Coarse fishermen may also like to know that many Welsh rivers hold stocks of coarse fish in the calmer downstream parts – even in the middle reaches sometimes. The Usk, Wye, Severn and Dee can be cited as notable examples.

These big rivers have another characteristic in common which holidaying anglers would do well to note. In their lower reaches there are many sections which can be hazardous to children and the elderly. High overhanging clay banks which can break away without warning if one ventures too close to the edge, for example. The lower Wye is the one to watch. This deep, powerful river has a great many long stretches where the water is compressed into a trough between high, slippery banks which plunge steeply into the water – and keep going down! It is only too easy to slide into deep, fast-flowing water with little prospect of getting ashore for a considerable distance downstream. Be careful, even in low water conditions!

As an aside, the recently completed barrage at the mouth of the Tawe in Swansea has retained several miles of calm water behind its bulk. Already several species of coarse fish have begun to thrive in this long, thin lake although what the effect will be on the migratory fish has yet to be determined. The local fishing clubs are still pessimistic about the prospects but it is to be hoped their gloom is misguided. So far the effects have been neutral if not beneficial. All being well, there may be a considerable gain in creating a coarse fishery where before there only used to be a foul-smelling trench, as well as retaining the excellent game fishing upstream. The matter is relevant when one considers the number of projected barrages in the planning stages across the country. Only time will tell whether they will prove to be a boon or an environmental disaster.

Any angler who takes his holiday near the lower reaches of one of the Welsh rivers is advised to pack tackle suitable for all sorts of fishing if he has no idea what he is going to find. Since the lower reaches are, by definition, near the coast, he should not forget his sea tackle if he does any sea fishing. Dry and wet fly, light and heavy spinning gear, live bait, all can provide good results if used in the appropriate water conditions. On subsequent visits to the same area it will be possible to leave much tackle at home as the best methods to use will have been learned by experience.

Waders, incidentally, are essential. So is a nice big bag to carry the catch and sandwiches, and for those not confident enough in their own ability to beach a ten pound (4.53 kg) salmon, a landing net is a very useful adjunct, even more so when fishing some distance from the nearest shelving bank. It can be extremely stressful struggling with a nice trout you wish to consume if you have to fight your way to a far bank over slippery pebbles in a wide, fast run. The potential meal usually ends up on someone else's plate another day.

Fishing at night can produce very good results, especially late in the season and if migratory fish are desired. Take a torch with good batteries if you wish to try this. Just take one night a couple of years ago, by no means untypical.

The rain had stopped mid-afternoon. It was now one o'clock in the morning and the angler knew he wouldn't get to sleep just yet so he set off for the road bridge over the river, taking his normal spinning tackle which consisted of a thirty-six year old, home-made, solid glass fibre rod, only four and a half feet (137 cm) long, and a Mitchell 300 fixed-spool reel of equal age.

The bridge over the spate river was also old. Single-track, triple-arched and leaning a little from the weight of traffic it was never designed to carry, it stood stolidly resisting the heavy water flow shoving at its twin masonry support pillars. A yellow street lamp at each end lit the scene. Huge sycamore trees stood on the opposite bank shedding their rain-sodden autumn leaves into water already crammed with them. A couple of tottering drunks supported each other over the bridge towards their homes and undoubtedly aggressive wives. The angler climbed down some huge stones protecting the bank from erosion and took up position at the waterside. A two inch (5.1 cm), plain silver Mepps with added weight was fitted to the eight pound (3.6 kg) line.

The bridge's twin pillars split the river into three equal parts, each of which had gouged a deep hollow immediately downstream of the bridge. The water level was high enough to cover the pebble banks thrown up in the lee of the pillars, these narrow, sheltered parts forming a strip of comparatively quiet water for twenty metres or so downstream. Tossing brown water rushed under the arches. To fall in was to die.

The street lamps threw plenty of light to facilitate accurate casting. Nothing much happened for the first half-hour – then a take was felt. The next cast, another one. Then another. A shoal of soft-mouthed sea-trout fresh from the sea was passing upstream. During the next twenty minutes several fish were lost. Finally one was landed, beached in a convenient gap between two wave-washed boulders. A nice sea-trout, it weighed about two pounds and used every ounce of it in the strong current, all to no avail. All went quiet for a while until a heavy weight bent the little rod into a straining bow. The relatively calm water behind the nearest pillar erupted as a large fish broke the surface and leapt into the air. Again and again it jumped. The old rod groaned in protest, the reel creaked and complained, the fish entered the current and raced downstream. Gone! Took the spinner with it too.

With the usual indecent utterances and hands trembling with emotion and the onset of blocked arteries, a fresh spinner was attached. Within a few minutes work had commenced once more. Almost immediately another snatch was felt as the spinner was drawn upstream close to the bank. Again the little rod bent to its work, slowly easing a substantial weight against the current. It felt flaccid, like a waterlogged branch, but gradually line was wound in until a large fish was discerned shimmering in the yellowish water at the angler's feet. He carefully entered the water, about eighteen inches (46 cm) deep at that point, and guided the unresisting fish to the gap in the boulders.

A salmon! About eight pounds (3.63 kg) and in fine condition. Not only that but another spinner dangled from its cavernous mouth next to the one that had caught it. Yes, you've guessed it, it was the very same spinner the angler had thought he'd lost shortly before. What a bonus, and how stupid can a fish get? Taking another chance like that only a few minutes after battling for life! Dumb fish – but very tasty.

The night's sport ended with an encounter with another shoal of sea-trout just after it began to pour with rain once more. Three more were caught; one retained for the freezer, the others returned to the water, and the angler went home to sleep off the excitement.

The narrow old bridge has gone now, replaced by a rather nice-looking, single-arched, wider structure. The number of road accidents has increased too, due to a greater sense of false security felt by motorists. The three pools have also gone, contractors having reneged on their promise to leave the stumps of the original pillars. All that is left is a constantly shifting run, shallow and unstable, whilst the few massive lumps of rock thrown in as an afterthought – and a sop to the protestations of the local angling club at the loss of some of their best pools – gradually sink beneath the rolling pebbles. Just another casualty of official vandalism.

Pity, really! But not all that unusual.

There is one little point that can make a big difference to an otherwise fishless day. All experienced anglers know that an east or north wind can put the kiss of death on a fish's appetite. An old, and not very good poem sums it up nicely:

When the wind is in the north
The prudent fisher goes not forth.
When the wind is in the south
It blows the bait into the fish's mouth.

No, it's not a very good poem, is it? Let's be honest, it's terrible, but the advice is generally correct though most of us can probably remember notable exceptions.

Now, except for the north coast and the border, most Welsh rivers flow generally to the south or west and when a north or east wind is blowing the flow of air is downstream. So it follows that a downstream wind ensures the fishing will not be up to much over most of the country. We've all experienced it; the fish simply don't seem to be interested in anything edible either on the surface or the bottom.

It would be a pity not to have at least a try down the river in such conditions as there are always exceptions, the contrary attitude of fish being what it is. You may possibly have a successful day but don't hold your breath! However, if it's as useless as expected, wait until the last couple of hours before sunset and then set off for the river again. The reason is as follows.

Whatever the direction of wind flow over the country, the land will always warm up faster than the sea even if the sun is continually hidden by clouds. Sea temperature rises throughout

Castell Malgwyn water on the lower Teifi. Salmon and sea trout from early on. Big, wild brownies, too.

the summer at a slow but inexorable rate and falls hardly at all during the course of a single night. As a result, the daytime land temperature, reaching its highest value a couple of hours before sunset, will always be above that of the sea during the summer months.

Warm air rises and creates a low pressure layer at ground level, the lowest relative pressure being at the bottom of the valleys. Air from the cooler sea flows up the valleys to maintain the balance. As long as the downstream wind is less than gale force, this sea-breeze will act in opposition to the wind blowing over the mountains and reverse or, at least, nullify its effect. The result is a slight upstream breeze even when a glance at the clouds overhead shows they are definitely moving in a downstream direction.

The fish won't care. As far as they are concerned the air flow is no longer in the wrong direction and they can come out to play without breaking the rules. And they do! Forced into a feeding shutdown during the whole of the day, fins and tail spring into quivering action and out come the fish, hungry and determined not to allow anything edible to get by them. A river which showed no signs of holding any fish whatsoever earlier in the day can boil with a feeding frenzy in the late evening and until well after dark as the inhabitants catch up on their dietary requirements.

This evening sea-breeze flows up all the valleys on the west and south-facing coasts where most of the Welsh rivers enter the sea; the nearer the coast the stronger the breeze. Depending on the length of the river, benevolent effects can be discerned in the middle and even the upper reaches of many rivers. A prudent fisherman will always bear this natural process in mind if the fishing is poor. So if the wind is coming from the wrong direction, and the fish are keeping their heads down, find something else to do during the daytime and reap the benefits of your foresight and knowledge in the late evening.

Anything good is worth waiting for!

Chapter 5

Lakes and Reservoirs

O bounteous quilt of water, rippling bright;
Your dim, green, weedy deeps concealed from sight,
Wherein my urgent effort concentrates
With rod, line, hook and several tasty baits.

Chris Thomas   1941-not dead yet!

TAKE ANOTHER LOOK at the Ordnance Survey map of the area where you intend spending your holiday and it is a fair bet there will be a very large number of lakes marked thereupon; big ones, small ones, some in between and others which are mere dots. In fact there are over 400 natural lakes and 90 reservoirs in Wales.

If you doubt these figures, count them yourself and add half the total plus a bit more. You may then be closer to the actual number because there are many more small still waters which are not yet marked or are too tiny to be on the map . These are the artificial pools and ponds scraped out of the ground by a mechanical digger and stocked with oversized brown and rainbow trout.

So there are, in effect, three different types of still water among the Welsh mountains; natural lakes, reservoirs and, for want of a more aesthetic description, battery fish-bowls. Consider the natural lakes to begin with.

The larger ones like Bala, Padarn and Cowlyd are not only nearly all accessible by road but also tend to be congregated in the northern half of the country, a result of the glacial processes already mentioned elsewhere. A few are extremely deep. Bala Lake (*Llyn Tegid*), for instance, is over 309 feet (94 metres) deep in places, while the mighty trough of Llyn Cowlyd hemmed in by its majestic cliffs plunges down 222 feet (67.67 metres) below the surface. It is alleged that the small, melancholy tarn of Dulyn (Black Lake), not far from Cowlyd, has been plumbed to 395 feet (120.4 metres) in one place without touching the bottom.

Anglers may find they will often have to share the larger, more easily accessible lakes with many other water sports such as sailing, wind surfing and motor-boats – even speedboats on some more popular waters. It can be difficult to find a peaceful and undisturbed section in the height of summer on either the shores or out on a boat. Not really to be recommended for those who seek tranquil surroundings. School holidays and fine weekends are the worst. Blissful peace will prevail at most other times.

Unfortunately the big lakes also hold some jolly good fish as well as being home to some rather unusual species. Llyn Padarn at Llanberis contains a lot of Arctic char – as do a couple of other lakes not very far away – while Bala Lake is nearly the only British water in which the *gwyniad* is to be found. A small salmonid, it spends its time in the deeper parts feeding on minute snails, insect larvae and water lobelia. It comes into shallow water to breed and only a few have ever been caught on a rod, deep nets being the only practical method. If you are lucky enough to capture one of these unusual fish please return it unharmed to the lake after taking a snap with your camera. They have been there since the Ice Age and it would be tragic if they were lost forever as a result of greed. So many other creatures have disappeared this way.

As long as you are patient and tolerant of the noisy habits of fellow human beings (natural attributes of the average angler), you should not find their presence on your chosen lake too infuriating. You can always get there first thing in the morning, pick a nice rainy day which will keep all but the most obsessed water-sporters away, or wait until they all go home in the evening. With a little bit of good fortune you will be able to accumulate a nice bagful of whatever you are trying to catch.

On the other hand, you may not wish to compete for space with others, especially if you live in a big town or city and want to get away from that sort of thing. In this case why not try one of the smaller lakes which nestle in profusion among the high peaks even if access proves a bit more difficult? This is not always the case, though. A great many have some form of vehicular access even if it is only a rutted track. Most are well worth a visit.

Certain angling clubs have supplemented the natural head of fish by stocking, and some memorable fishing can be found if a visit is made in the right conditions. Obviously stocking cannot be carried out unless a fish tanker can get to the waterside so you will often find that a lake both managed by a club and with road access will have a useful number of worthwhile fish bumbling around the place.

The remainder of the natural lakes – those not managed by a club and which have to be reached on foot or by helicopter – provide a mixture of angling qualities ranging from the lifelessness of acid water to burgeoning vitality. Some have never in living memory held fish , such as Llyn y Fan Fawr in the Brecon Beacons, while others have been despoiled by acid rain and even wiped out completely. The only way to find out for sure is to go and see. Travel light, take account of the weather and act accordingly.

As an aside, two small lakes may possess an added attraction for those with a penchant for the unusual. One is Llyn Dywarchen at the side of the B4418 near Rhyd-ddu. There used to be a floating island wandering around this irregularly-shaped lake, pushed hither and thither by the strong winds which blow in this elevated position. It was known to be there at the beginning of the 20th century but alas is no more. Theories for its disappearance range from the development of a puncture to the more probable one of vandalism.

The other is called Llyn y Pysgod Un Llygad (Lake of the One-eyed Fish). Ancient rumour asserts there was a lake high in the mountains of Gwynedd containing three species of fish: trout, perch and eels. All living in this lake had only one eye – the right one. Unfortunately the exact location remains unknown, though it has been suggested Ffynnon Llugwy Reservoir under one of the mighty southern shoulders of Carnedd Llywelyn may have been the site. Or it might have been Llyn y Foel? Or perhaps. . . ?

Anyway, now for the reservoirs. Some are natural lakes which have been enlarged and deepened by building a shallow retaining

Tal-y-llyn Lake, 220 acres full of fish. To be recommended.

wall while others are deliberately drowned valleys and completely artificial like those in the Elan Valley. The increasing need for extra water by a modern society means more and more is being extracted from the Welsh mountains. Luckily this is now being done in a more sensitive manner than in days gone by. The use of rivers as pipelines and pumping stations as distribution systems enables the water to be kept in the rivers to a greater extent than if the water were simply transported through underground pipes from the reservoirs.

This practice creates the apparent anomaly of relatively high water in a river flowing from a dam when all the surrounding rivers are suffering from drought conditions. The Usk is a case in point together with the Dee, Severn, Ystwyth and several others. It is a strange sensation coming to one of these rivers after weeks without rain and finding it high and coloured. The trout love it, though, and respond with enthusiasm and a collective death-wish. The volume of water released is rarely enough to provide a fully-fledged flood except for the stretch immediately below the dam but there is always sufficient to galvanize the underwater inhabitants into a feeding frenzy for a long way downstream. When wading in a river of this sort it is wise to be sharply aware of any increase in the height or colour of the water around you and beat a hasty retreat to safety on the most convenient bank if it begins to rise.

Most major reservoirs are stocked with fish by the controlling water authority or sub-let to private interests. The quality of fishing is nearly always excellent, many reservoirs also holding large stocks of coarse fish, such as Llyn Alaw on the island of Anglesey and Trawsfynydd Lake, but few attempts have been made to develop this side of the fishing tracks. Indeed, to the horror of a great many coarse anglers, it is sometimes requested, and in some cases mandatory, to deliberately kill any coarse fish caught in order to improve the game fishing qualifications of the water. In these supposedly enlightened times there are many who would say this kind of thing should not happen. There is no logical reason why game and coarse fish cannot cohabit and thereby allow anglers of either persuasion to reap the benefits (and pay the ticket fees).

A cynic may feel obliged to point out that coarse fishing does not produce the same revenue (i.e. profit) as game fishing. A casual study of the ticket pricing arrangements would tend to reinforce this view. In the absence of any obviously valid arguments to the contrary, the cynic may well be right, which is a terrible shame for the innocent coarse fish.

Many reservoirs provide boats for the use of those who wish to get well away from the shore line. If you wish to avail yourself of one of these it would be sensible to book well in advance as it is sometimes the case that they are all in use. At the same time as booking, find out about any restrictions on their use and whether you are expected to bring any extra equipment (e.g. your own life jacket).

Because these reservoirs are much in demand for competition angling it can be a good idea to ascertain whether one is to be held on the day you wish to fish or you might find yourself shoulder to shoulder with hordes of eager contestants flogging the water to a foam. They always head for the best bits, too. Gregariousness is an admirable human trait but it can sometimes be stretched to the limit of tolerance during such times.

A similar situation can exist on the battery fish-ponds. Because these are invariably commercial enterprises, the maximum number of anglers will be packed on to the minimum length of bank for the maximum price sustainable. A friendly attitude is not only advised – it is essential. The rewards, however, can be spectacular. Where else can you have a chance at beaching a trout of 20 lbs (9.07 kg) in weight? Not in any Welsh river, that's for sure. Or any other in the UK, come to that.

Of course, these huge fish grow to such an unnatural size because they are fed artificially with high-protein pellets. They have to be, because the shallow scrapes in the ground in which they are forced to spend their pallid and sluggish lives are simply not big enough to supply sufficient food to maintain their requirements from natural local resources.

There are a great many of these battery fish-bowls scattered all over Wales and no doubt a great many more will appear in the future in places where there is a source of clean, fresh water and a sympathetic planning committee. The holiday angler will almost certainly have a choice of several venues of this type to choose from wherever he may stay. As long as the expense of fishing this type of water is considered to be justified, one day can always be set aside to sample the produce. At the very least it will serve to increase one's enjoyment of other waters where the fish roam untamed and free from the confines of a small, enclosed pond.

These fish farms have another benefit to the river angler. For every customer who spends his time (and cash) in a fish farm a gap is created on the river bank. Pressure for river space is thereby diminished and the river angler is more likely to have an undisturbed day out instead of competing with others for the available fish.

There is a certain area in south Wales where a reservoir has been stocked with brown and rainbow trout; in an adjoining valley lies another reservoir which has been abandoned owing to flooding into a coal mine. This second reservoir now only retains a small, circular pool, about 50 yards (45.7 metres) across, behind the huge barrier of the dam which stands across the narrow valley as a gaunt, grey monument to redundancy. Just a couple of miles away a battery fish-pond has been scraped out of a green field and offers fish-flesh for the freezer – at a price and if you can catch it yourself. Close by, a small country pub served as a place of refreshment for three fishermen who happened to meet one evening a few years ago, each having sampled the delights of one of the venues mentioned above that very day.

The first angler to arrive immediately began pouring best bitter down his throat and considered he had experienced a pretty good day out at the fish farm sharing a small pond with nine other anglers. Two big rainbow trout, flabby and already starting to go off, languished in a plastic bag at the base of his bar stool. Although the pub was only a very short distance from the fish farm, their combined weight of just over fourteen pounds (6.35 kg) had taken its toll of his remaining stamina and it seemed the best way to replenish it was to have a couple of refreshing jugs before lugging them to his home a few doors away.

When he was well into his second glass of gargle the other two anglers arrived together and joined him to compare notes. To the surprise of the few other customers angler 1 proudly displayed his victims. The landlord whispered a few words gently into his ear. The fish were concealed once more. The landlord wiped the slimy drips off his spotless bar top then ostentatiously sprayed the air with a small can of deodoriser.

"Nice ones, those," said angler 2. "Got them at the farm, yes?"

"Both on an Alder, size 10. Hooked another two a bit smaller afterwards but lost 'em both. Just as well, really. Didn't have enough cash on me to weigh them in. Still, these'll do me. How've you done?"

"Been up the reservoir, me. Had a good few. I'd 've stayed a bit longer and maybe got a few more but me mate here arrived to pick me up so I packed it in."

"How many, then?"

"Oh, six nice ones on the bank and double that lost. About sixteen pounds (7.26 kg) of fish altogether. Quite a day, all told, and never had to change the flies once. Black and Silver did all the real work. Good fly that, up there, 'specially when it's a bit dull and cloudy like now."

Anglers 1 and 2 nodded wisely at each other. Both were experienced and quite used to catching plenty of big fish. Angler 3 grabbed two full pint glasses from the barman and buried his nose in one of them. His Adam's apple jiggled wildly for a few moments before he resurfaced, gasping, like a walrus breaking through the ice. The other pint was handed to angler 2 and the performance was repeated – with the addition of a few personal variations. Angler 1 nudged angler 3.

"What about you, then? Didn't bother today, eh?"

"Went up the old drained reservoir." Angler 3 reached into an armpit and scratched vigorously. "Damned place is full of mosquitoes."

Now that it had been mentioned, angler 1 noticed a large number of discoloured patches in various stages of development all over angler 3's face and neck. A transparent drip, tinged with beer and nicotine, hung from one nostril like a small pendant and he was soaking wet up to waist level. The odour of mud and rotting waterweed surrounded him like an aura.

"Fell in too?" enquired angler 1 sympathetically.

"Happens every time I go up there," muttered angler 3 in a faint, despairing voice. "Edges are all muddy weed floating on the surface. Then it drops off suddenly into deep water, but it's worth it."

Angler 2 chipped in,

"Don't know why he bothers with the place, myself. Fish up there aren't worth catching. I keep telling him but he won't listen."

"Well for a start it doesn't cost anything." Angler 3 was stung into self-defence. His status as a fisherman was in danger of being undermined. "Nobody else ever goes there so I've got the place to myself and there's plenty of fish always rising to anything I offer them. It suits me fine."

"How many are you taking home, then?" asked angler 1.

"None. Never do."

"So you spent all day up there and never caught anything?"

"Course not. Caught quite a few. Always do." He guzzled more beer to emphasise the fact.

"How many?"

"Didn't count but must have been well over thirty."

"All small 'uns, eh?"

"Had one about half a pound (227 grams) but the rest were small. Put them all back."

"Waste of time, then. I like to take a couple home."

"Agreed." said angler 2. "I keep telling him but he never takes any notice. Ready for another round?"

The point of this little conversation is that there is a niche for anglers of all types and persuasion, all with differing requirements, within the list of Welsh still-waters. The three anglers above all knew one another well and respected one another's preferences without either serious disparagement or agreement. There is room for all, and if your holiday simply isn't long enough you can always come back again to try the bits you missed.

There is one further bit of information which may be of interest to the holiday angler who goes equipped for all types of fishing, and it is to do with the multitude of small streams flowing into most of the lakes.

Late in the season, from about mid-August onwards, the urge falls upon all trout to migrate upstream and do the necessary things to ensure the continuance of their species. In the interests of maintaining a sex-free publication (and in spite of such practices normally being considered an essential part of any modern

Llyn Padarn for trout, salmon, sea trout and Arctic char amid spectacular Snowdon scenery. Boats available.

narration), their activities on the spawning grounds will be left for discussion by more specialized and learned texts in both soft or hard porn format. All that is important here is the fact that lake trout are subject to the same compulsions and unless they want to do it in the lake they will have to go and find a suitable stream.

Most lakes will only have a selection of small brooks from which to choose, the one occupying the main valley being the biggest. The trout will have to make do with these, and at the right time of the year, if there is enough rainfall to give a decent water flow, a large number of very big lake trout can be found in pools of a quite disproportionate size. The author recently witnessed a heron capturing a trout weighing well over a pound (454 grams) alongside a main road in a stream only a few inches deep and no more than two feet (61 cm) wide. It was early December and the lake into which the stream flowed was only a quarter of a mile (.4 km) downstream. A big fish in a little pond in truth!

Late in the season, after rain and when the water is relatively high, is the time to fish these lake-feeding brooks with a worm, preferably a medium-sized lob, on a size 6 or 4 hook. That's the *best* time, maybe, but don't let an absence of such conditions keep you from trying anyway. To stalk and successfully land a plump, glittering two pounder (907 grammer) from a tiny, grass-lined pool containing scarcely enough depth of water to cover its back is an experience not to be forgotten.

Although only a small proportion of the latter part of the season will give a chance of catching these big lake trout in such places, it is strongly advised to have a go if you are staying near, or fishing, a suitable lake. The results can often fully compensate for a bad day on larger waters.

Chapter 6

Welsh Coarse Fishing

Hence comes great store, and various kinds of fish,
So good as may enrich the empty dish.

Rowland Watkyns   1635-1664

A GREAT MANY coarse fishermen from over the border seem to have a bit of trouble associating Wales with any prospect of acceptable angling rewards. Not so many years ago they may have had a point but the situation is completely different now.

During those unenlightened times, simple apathy and the preponderance of good game fishing kept the spirit and practice of coarse angling in the hands of just a few keen individuals. Many good venues were neglected, poisoned by the redistribution of industrial wastes or used as land-fill sites for the disposal of rubble and domestic refuse.

This is still happening today, although on a greatly reduced scale, environmental awareness even now being considered subordinate to commercial interests and the local jobs they may possibly create. On the bright side, new coarse fisheries are actually being started up in some places.

The most prolific area for coarse fishing venues is

undoubtedly in the south of the country and along much of the border with England. From the rivers Wye and Usk in the east, across the coastal plain of Gwent and Glamorgan, up to the Heads of the Valleys road (A465) high on the Brecon Beacons and right the way across to near the Irish Sea in Dyfed (home to the famed waterlily-laden Bosherton Lakes), there are ponds, canals, lakes and a few big rivers holding coarse fish in enough numbers and of a size to satisfy the most sophisticated of coarse anglers.

Mid Wales has rather fewer places where coarse fish are to be found. There are several, however, in both rivers and some lakes. The river Severn and its tributaries together with parts of the upper Wye have a monopoly of moving water venues and are rich with many species from small dace to specimen pike. Lakes such as Llangorse and the popular well-managed lake at Llandrindod Wells hold a large stock of fish. There are several smaller ones as well, both natural and artificial. The Shropshire Union canal running from Newtown right down to and through Chester can provide excellent fishing as well as its spur running up the Dee valley to Llangollen. As an example, a carp weighing close to eleven kilograms has recently been caught close to Buttington's Wharf east of Welshpool.

Mid-Wales also has several rivers such as the Wye and upper Severn together with their tributaries in which the grayling may be found. Fine fishing may be experienced with a fly on the right day in the depths of winter for this worthy species.

North Wales also has its share of the sport (including grayling) in the shape of the Dee, all the way from near its source in Bala Lake right down to the tidal reaches below Chester. Westwards of here the only worthwhile coarse fishing is to be found in just a few small ponds – at least until the island of Anglesey is reached.

Anglesey is the driest and sunniest part of Wales with an average rainfall of close to thirty inches (76 cm) and 1,500 hours of sunshine. There are quite a lot of useful venues for an angler staying in the island's 280 square miles (725 sq km) of gently undulating countryside – and some are free of ticket fees. There are several pretty big lakes too, a couple of which hold trout as well as several coarse species.

But what can the holiday coarse angler realistically expect to catch in Welsh waters?

Just about anything, really, unless his consuming passion happens to be barbel, although it is said even these are still to be found in the Severn since their experimental introduction some time in the early '70s. The author respectfully declines to substantiate these rumours in the absence of any personal sightings but hopes that any still there will thrive and prosper.

Suffice to say that roach, rudd and perch are to be found in just about any coarse water. Pike are on the increase, encroaching relentlessly upon water previously free of these ruthless and gluttonous predators (no doubt with a little assistance in the matter of transport by pike fanatics). Carp and tench, some of considerable bulk, can be found in certain places in south and mid-Wales. So can bream – a relatively new immigrant to Welsh waters – and chub seem to like living in large numbers in the eastern rivers, even right up in the head-waters of some of the slower-flowing tributaries.

Grayling have already been mentioned as being fully paid-up and historical residents of the Wye, Severn and Dee. Rising energetically to a dry fly (or snatching a wet one just as quickly when in the mood) this coarse fish is a favourite for sporting pursuit during the winter months. It must be mentioned, though, that some waters are shut down completely in winter to give all members of the salmon family peace to properly perform their procreative duties.

In spite of this, there is no reason why the holiday angler should not take advantage of the lower accommodation tariffs and less crowded water offered during the off-peak season. If grayling is the quarry it is best to ascertain that grayling fishing is available before booking.

A good time to try is after the end of the trout fishing season in October. Not only will you have the chance of a fine catch but the weather during this part of the year is inclined to be relatively mellow (with a little luck), the grayling are in fine shape, and fly hatches can still be abundant. Another advantage is that there is still a good chance of catching a salmon on some waters before the migratory fish season ends. There are still likely to be plenty of leaves on the trees which is a great asset when it comes to avoiding tangles and losses of tackle due to unnoticed twigs and branches. The countryside looks at its best when dressed in autumnal livery, too.

In certain grayling fishing stretches there will be sizeable populations of perch, roach, rudd, dace or gudgeon as well, all of which will take a fly at times although, with the exception of perch which possess a politician-sized mouth, a very small fly will be needed. Low water is obviously required to gain the maximum benefit from fly fishing for these species but if a selection of tackle is taken the methods of capture can be varied at will whatever the circumstances.

Most of the main coarse fisheries in Wales have been in existence for many thousands of years, notably those in the large reed-lined lakes such as Llangorse and Bala, or the big rivers like the Wye and Usk, and things haven't really changed all that much in the meantime. Proof of this is to be found in Bala Lake, for instance, where the herring-like *gwyniad* can be found, resident there since the Ice Age and still going strong. Very deep ledgering from a boat will be required to tempt one of these along with small, specialized baits and an enormous amount of good fortune. They enter shallow water during their breeding season but tend not to feed at such times – their minds being concentrated on things other than food.

It's not really worth attempting to catch one of these shy fish to the exclusion of all the other species Bala Lake has to offer. A net is the only practical way of doing so, anyway. Their numbers are not large and they tend to stay in the deepest water. And bits of Bala Lake are *very* deep. If you do happen to catch one accidentally, please return it to the lake unharmed. Life is precarious enough for them without us anglers making it even more insecure.

The picture is rather different in the south-eastern valleys where things are altering much more rapidly than elsewhere. Even more dramatic changes are planned for the future, as public opinion exerts pressure upon the "powers that be" to be sensitive to the environment whenever they exercise their planning prerogatives. Industrial and residential developers are gradually being dragged grizzling and kicking into the twenty-first century, more conscious of their responsibility to the surroundings and wildlife than ever before.

It is in the old industrial and coal mining valleys where improvements are at their most dramatic. Obviously intrusive coal tips have been all but eradicated. Rivers have been cleaned up and ponds and canals restored to a state of health far exceeding that which existed when they were used for industrial purposes. This is not to say that some smaller pools have not fallen victim to the desire to build a housing estate, a supermarket or a factory, but the river authority is on the ball these days, ensuring there is minimal loss of fish stocks and arranging for their relocation when necessary.

By far the best example of this is to be found in the lower Swansea valley, south of the M4, where not so many years ago the whole valley floor resembled one of the more hostile regions of the lunar landscape. The area has recently been transformed into a bustling trading estate retaining many of the best original waterside features. A lake and several ponds have been cleaned up. All hold fish and provide a home for several species of waterfowl. Even better, due to the construction of access roads, these waters are now accessible to anglers who are not as active as they used to be. Wheelchair fishermen will find many safe pitches.

In addition to this, a barrage has been constructed across the river mouth where it enters the dockyards creating a forty-foot (12.2 metre) deep lake. Instead of a muddy tidal trench three miles (5 km) in length there now exists a narrow lake full of fresh water. A few species of coarse fish, including chub, are beginning to occupy this long, thin waterway and there is every reason to believe this will become an extremely important coarse fishery in the near future.

From poison and filth to prolific waters. A benevolent transformation indeed!

So it can easily be seen that not all alterations are for the worse. A similar scene is being enacted all over south Wales among the grey, crumbling ruins of its industrial heritage. Some small local venues are being eliminated while others are being opened up, cleaned out or newly created. Water management authorities are active in monitoring transfer and stocking of fish and ensuring all the ingredients are in place for their survival. They do a pretty good job of it too, within the boundaries of their financial capabilities. Many coarse fishing clubs have been formed in the last twenty years thereby ensuring proper treatment of the waters and nearly all are prepared to issue tickets to visiting anglers.

Overall, the situation has greatly improved and the future for coarse fishing in Wales can be viewed with justifiable optimism.

It follows that wherever the holiday coarse angler decides to stay, especially in south Wales, there should be a good coarse fishery not very far away, perhaps several, but there is one point which should never be ignored or left to chance: the availability of bait!

There are very few places in Wales where fresh supplies of ground bait, worms, maggots or other tasties can be obtained without perhaps having to travel a considerable distance to obtain them. Don't rely on luck! Always take enough with you to last the whole of your holiday unless you can definitely locate a reliable and convenient source of supply.

The Shropshire Union Canal basin at Froncysyllte alongside its famous lofty aqueduct. Excellent carp and tench here besides most other coarse species.

Fresh live-bait able to wriggle or crawl without assistance is the main problem – maggots, in particular. It is recommended you treat some nice fresh ones to a holiday in your company. The casters into which they evolve can still be useful during the final few days. A couple of weeks is just not long enough to create your own supply by means of a limp lump of rotten meat hanging outside your door on a piece of string. Landlords of holiday premises tend not to be over-keen on this practice, either.

Worms are notorious for being hard to find when you need them. If you think you will be using them it is worth taking a good supply with you, whether you are hoping to catch coarse or game fish. Of course they are unlikely to last a full week in hot weather without turning into a tepid and aromatic worm soup so you may have to obtain them locally. A chat with the local farmer may be productive. You can then either search his cow-shed waste heap or look around his fields. This can be great fun at night using a torch and a soft footstep.

For the sake of those unfamiliar with this challenging but entrancing pastime, this is how to do it. Go out into the field or garden just after it goes dark armed with a good flashlight and a jam-jar (thoroughly washed and empty of jam – worms do not seem to like any of today's flavours). Best results are obtained when the ground is wet or when a heavy dew is settling. Tread gently and slowly over the grass, eyes alert for the quarry, until a worm is spotted lying full length (the only way worms can lie) across the greensward enjoying a moonbath or just relaxing after a hard day's work. Keep the potential victim in view on the periphery of the lit circle being careful not to allow the full beam on its skin or it may quickly dodge back into its hidy-hole.

Pick out the reddest end, this will be the head, and gradually reach down with the hand not holding the flashlight to the other end (the tail). A short section of this tail will usually still be poked inside the hole from which the worm has just emerged. With a fast snatch, grab the creature as close as possible to its bolt-hole between thumb and forefinger and lift it up. You will have to be pretty quick and will often have to work the worm from its lair by pulling gently. The pain from broken fingernails and damaged cuticles must be ignored at all costs.

Worms are quiet creatures. They never scream even when wrenched violently from their homes. This useful inhibition ensures any others in the immediate vicinity will not be alarmed unless you start flashing the light around or stamping with excitement at your success. Place your victim in the jam-jar with a little grass to keep it happy (natural and fresh from the field – not the sort which is smoked) and go on searching and seizing until you have enough for the following day's fishing.

Catching worms in this manner can often be more exciting than the fishing on the day they are used but just be careful where you do it. Ask for permission, if necessary, and don't use the local park or village green in case of ghastly mis-understandings. Down by the river bank is not a good place, either. Local bailiffs are rarely amused at being dragged away from the telly to answer the report of a light being used by suspected poachers down by the river, only to find a tourist with a jar of traumatised worms and an unlikely explanation.

Most other live baits can be obtained when actually on the water. Slugs for the big Severn and Wye chub? Just rummage around rotten wood or stones in the undergrowth or offer to be the local allotment club's slug-buster on a temporary basis. The same with snails. Small fish to be used as live bait for pike can be caught freshly on the day they are required but allow some extra time for this as they can sometimes be more elusive than the quarry they are meant to tempt. Doubts about one's ability in this field can be resolved by a visit to the wet-fish shop for small whole mackerel, herring or sprats. But these are an inferior substitute as any pike-man will tell you.

In extremity, the hedgerows and woods can be scoured for juicy organisms that crawl or wriggle. Just stay clear of things that can bite or inject painful toxins into your tender flesh and remember the old belief, never disproved satisfactorily, that if bait is hard to get then the fishing is bound to be good.

Bread paste, cheese, rice, corned beef, maize, potatoes, pasta, sausage meat or other forms of junk-bait can always be picked up at the local grocers. Unfortunately, if these do not produce results you will naturally be convinced things would have been different if only you had proper live offerings with which to tempt the fish. Not easy to prove wrong this, is it?

Imagine a favourable weather forecast in mid-autumn. Dry, warm and sunny, hardly any wind – and what there is will be coming from the west. Expected morning mist clearing early. What a perfect time to try a Welsh lake for a mixed bag of coarse fish with the emphasis on the tench this particular lake is reputed to contain.

A certain fisherman decided to take the opportunity offered by this promising forecast and went to the lake after work one Friday armed with the business end of an old garden rake and a length of stout cord. Two holes were cleared among the water lilies thronging the lower end of the lake where a small dam about six feet (1.83 metres) high held the water in place. The openings were then laced thoroughly with ground-bait and the lake left to its overnight slumbers.

The waters behind the dam were only about 6 acres (2.43 hectares) in extent with a small, bushy island in the centre. Nowhere was it more than six feet (1.83 metres) deep over the soft mud bottom, and even better, few fished there. The characteristic signs of tench had been noticed on previous visits. They were there now – constant streams of slow-bursting bubbles trickling to the surface all over the place as though a convention of diminutive scuba-divers was in progress. Not a single tench had ever been actually seen by our angler.

Tackle was set up; a powerful three metre hollow glass fibre salmon fly rod fitted with a 4 inch (10 cm) centre-pin reel full of 7lb (3.18 kg) nylon, small quill running-float, no weights and a size 4 hook. The brand-new keep-net was carefully placed in the lake and a short trip undertaken round the water's edge at the side of the dam to search for bait. The angler had once been told that tench went wild over the slightest hint of a swan mussel. He collected a couple from the mud, opened and sliced one, then put the unprepossessing snack onto the hook with some difficulty.

Less than five minutes after casting out, the float keeled over on its side, bobbed upright again then commenced a slow and deliberate sideways slide under the surface. The angler counted slowly up to five then tightened firmly. A solid resistance was felt – too solid – like a water-logged timber, then the rod bent further and further as whatever was on the other end bored powerfully towards the safety of the massed water lilies.

It went into them! Ten minutes of cursing, sweating and trembling attempts at untangling finally unwound the line from the rubbery stems and a thick, dark shape lay sullenly at the edge of the dam. The landing net came into play.

A nice tench weighing in at four pounds (1.82 kg) it was. It didn't seem fair to consign such a magnificent fish to the imprisonment of a keep-net so it was released further along the dam wall. This particular angler's first tench!

The swan mussel looked untouched – tough bait, swan mussel – so it was used again and within a further ten minutes another tench found itself in a compromising position. Even bigger, this one. It weighed in at a shade under five pounds (2.26 kg) The angler felt faint with emotion and again returned it to the water with the respect it deserved.

In the two hours before the heat and strengthening brightness of the rising sun signalled to the tench that it was time to knock off work for the day, a total of eleven fine specimens had been taught that swan mussel can be hazardous to the health; the biggest being the five pounder (2.26 kg-er) caught early on and the smallest a comparative tiddler of 2lb (907 grams). It was much too early to go home so the angler put on a smaller hook and chopped the remaining mussel into little pieces.

The next three hours produced a catch of almost 14 lbs (6.36 kg) of roach, rudd and perch which would have overloaded the keep-net if it had been used. These included a roach of 1lb 12oz (795 grams), a rudd of 1lb 13oz (823 grams) and a beautiful perch of 2lb 12oz (1.249 kg). All these fish and the tench captured earlier on just three swan mussels and a few big lob-worms scratched up from the woodland vegetation when the mussels ran out. A good day all round by any standards.

An attempted re-run the following day in identical conditions only produced a few small apathetic and suicidal red-fins (roach, rudd and perch), but that's fishing, ain't it?

So if you are a keen coarse angler contemplating a stay of a week or two in Wales, don't leave your tackle at home or you could miss out on some extremely energetic sport. Maybe there are bigger fish back home, somewhere, but it is just possible a huge pike, tench or Llandrindod Wells Lake carp with a Welsh accent may have your number stamped on its side.

It would be a pity to disappoint it, don't you think?

There is free fishing at the present time in Llandrindod Wells lake. Plenty of perch, roach, rudd, tench, etc. Some specimen carp have been landed here.

Chapter 7

Welsh Sea Angling

Now all is still yet, ere today is done,
Where now these fairy runnels thread the sand
Five fathoms deep the swelling tides shall run.

Sir Lewis Morris   1833-1907

THE SALT-WATER ANGLER on a Welsh holiday will find his needs well catered for both in choice of places to have a go and in varieties of fish. From a coastline of nearly 733 miles (1180 kms), 17% of the total for Britain, there should be several favourable venues close to wherever it is decided to set up a base. A further bonus is that Welsh seaside towns are well endowed with tackle shops for the replacement of lost or forgotten items of sea tackle as well as providing useful local information and sometimes a supply of fresh bait.

To paint a proper picture we shall split Wales into three stretches of coast; the south, the west and the north. There are distinct differences in these three divisions as well as many similarities.

Take the south Wales coastline to begin with.

From the muddy reaches east of Cardiff to the Atlantic rollers pounding the scenic yellow Pembroke storm beaches, this length of coastline is dominated by the influence of the Severn estuary. West of Swansea the coastal scenery is of surpassing splendour, the Gower peninsular holding the richly deserved honour of being designated the first area of outstanding natural beauty in Britain. The National Trust controls much of the coastline and local planning authorities are keen to restrict anything which is likely to spoil the tourist industry upon which this part of Wales relies heavily.

The further east of Swansea you go, the more you have to be aware of the tide because this great cleft in the land is subjected to one of the biggest tidal ranges in the world, topped only by the Bay of Fundy across the Atlantic. During the spring tides it can rise over 44 feet (13.4 metres) above low water mark.

In view of this it can be seen that a certain degree of caution needs to be taken if you are not familiar with such conditions. Those who fish the vast beaches of East Anglia or places like Morcambe Bay where the tide retreats almost out of sight will be able to judge the safety aspect quite well, but if you habitually fish the steep beaches of the south east where there is often deep water just a few metres out, then a few words of advice will not be out of place.

Firstly, wherever you stay, go down to the beach you intend to try, when the tide is fully out. You may well find that there is a huge expanse of flat sand braided with shallow stretches of water dotted among the sandbanks. Typical examples are Broughton Bay at the end of the Gower peninsula and the areas each side of the Towy estuary. These places can be *dangerous!* Give them a miss until the tide is at least half way in, or you may find yourself unable to beat the encroaching waters and most of your fishing time will be spent rushing back and forth relocating your rods and tackle supplies. Neap tides, when the lower tidal range permits the beach to be covered at a more manageable rate, are a lot safer.

Still take care, though! Don't take small children right out at low tide; it is only too easy to become marooned on a sandbank and even the neap tide currents can be fierce enough to sweep you off your feet.

Most Welsh beaches, at least those which go out a long way, don't fish very well until three hours either side of high tide. This is not so much of a disadvantage as may be supposed because fresh local bait is more easily located and dug at low tide and a little planning will enable you to start fishing at the best time immediately after amassing the bait, thus avoiding both wasted time and a double trip.

In the height of summer there is one more major disadvantage in going to many of the more popular beaches to try your luck – other trippers who don't fish. They swim instead, or race around on jet-skis, slide through the surf on over-priced bits of plank, lie on the sand getting cooked, or simply gather around any angler who just wants to be left alone and is getting heartily sick of answering the eternal question "Caught anything yet?" Hyper-gregarious individuals may be able to cope with this aggravation but for most of us it is more likely to result in high blood pressure disorders and a rabid hatred of all mankind and his works. Better to go when the weather is bad, in the early morning or after dark, equipped with Tilley lamp and torches. Or you could try a less populated venue.

That's the trouble with the more accessible beaches – too

many people are able to get there and the fishing suffers accordingly. Still, there's plenty of choice in south Wales. Some beaches are so big that almost any number of people and activities can be accommodated. Look in at Cefn Sidan west of Llanelli, Pendine, Newgale or Llangennith and you will see! There are also many coves and small beaches scattered all along the coast, some of which are a bit hard to get to and consequently relatively unpopulated.

The bottom line is this: check out your chosen beach carefully before actually fishing there to avoid disappointment. If it's not up to scratch or seems likely to invite a battle for space with other holiday-makers, look elsewhere! You shouldn't have to go far afield.

The whole coastline is not sandy beach, there are plenty of good rock stands as well. Exploration at low tide is often necessary for the newcomer to discover the type of bottom, how far the tide retreats and the best escape route if bad weather blows up. Good rock ledges are to be found at Ogmore-by-Sea, the south face of the Gower peninsula, and to the west of Tenby although they are also to be found in many other locations. A chat with the local tackle dealer is well advised. Then check out your prospective stand for accessibility and any hazards to be negotiated if a steep cliff climb has to be undertaken, especially if there is a possibility of having to find your way back after dark.

There are surprisingly few piers in this part of the country and those which do exist are either subject to enough restrictions to dampen the enthusiasm of any serious fisherman or so plagued with mooring lines for the benefit of the boating brigade that an infinite supply of replacement weights and hooks is a necessity. Do not plan your fishing ventures around the availability of a problem-free pier.

Of course you may be a member of that self-same boating brigade, in which case you may be taking your boat on holiday with you. Any sensible boater will naturally take the trouble to find out about the nearest launching slip before committing himself. South Wales has plenty, as well as a lot of beaches convenient for the launch of a dinghy or small craft. Most launch points will have a choice of several good marks within a short steaming distance. Conversation with other boaters at the slipway will soon make you familiar with the local situation and the better-known marks. If they don't produce results find your own marks and keep your mouth shut about the best ones, just like everyone else.

What are you likely to catch? Nearly everything you can find elsewhere on the British coast, actually. Since most anglers take their holidays during the summer months it may be best to start with the fish available then.

From about the beginning of June, as the inshore water begins to warm up, salmon bass wander in close to the shoreline, either in shoals of fish up to two pounds (907 g) in weight or more solitary big 'uns up to ten pounds (4.54 kg) or more.

Bass are a Welsh speciality and they taste lovely. The thundering surf of the big storm beaches is the best place to find them although there are plenty nuzzling their way around the rocks beneath beetling cliffs in pursuit of succulent crabs and small fish. Their dietary preferences are quite wide but baits of lugworm, ragworm, sandeel or soft crab will nearly always produce results when a hungry bass is in the vicinity. Those who have never landed a bass should be careful about handling them; the spines on the dorsal fin and the razor-sharp edges of the gill covers could inflict a painful wound which can take a long time to heal.

Next, the ubiquitous flounder, found in any river estuary like that of the Loughor near Llanelli, the Conway, or the Towy below Carmarthen. Pick a time when the tides are relatively slack (not too large a rise between low and high tides) or the currents will be too strong to allow your weight to hold the bottom and the fish will scoot by too fast to grab your bait. In the event of high tides, try the two hours either side of low, or preferably high, tide when the race has slackened. Again, lug or rag is recommended, not least because bass also run up the estuaries with the tide to inspect the muddy channels among the salt flats for easy pickings. Flounders can sometimes be found in big groups on the muddier patches.

At the time of writing, three estuaries have been designated as nursery areas for salmon bass. These are the Dovey, Mawddach and Dwyryd/Glaslyn inlets where no bass may be fished for from a boat under pain of severe penalty. Shore fishing is allowed for this species in nursery areas, but it is expected that true sportsmen will respect the spirit and intention of this regulation and return, unharmed, any bass they happen to catch.

Plaice can also be found where there is a sandy bottom, either in an estuary or on the beach, but their movement into such shallow water is inclined to be patchy; after a storm is often a good time as is down at the low tide mark. Use baits as for bass.

The above three species are the most common to be caught

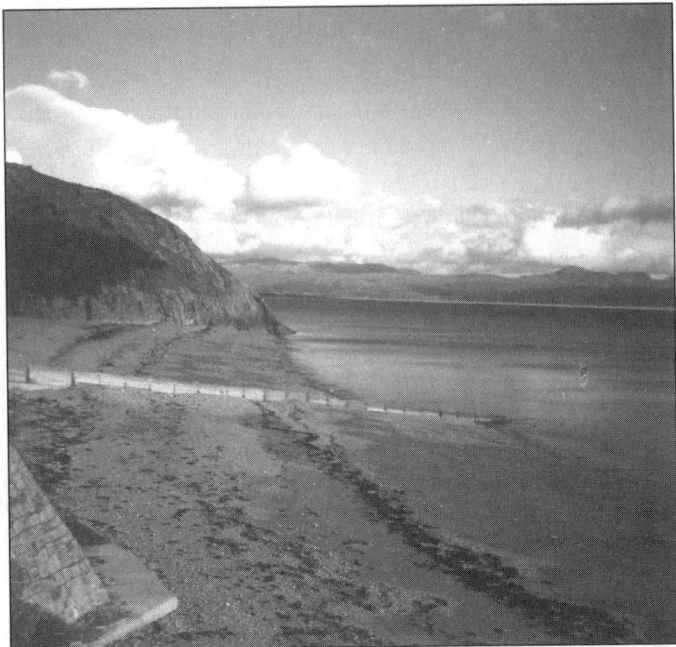

A steep pebble beach under the castle rock at Cricieth. Good current on the making tide brings mackerel and salmon bass past at the trot.

over sand and mud, although many places can produce a bag of dabs or sole when conditions are right. Pollack and pouting, of course, are everywhere. Mostly around the rocks, they can often turn up in the surf in large numbers, especially where there is a deep-water channel within casting distance. Summer time can often bring rather exotic species to our shores but it is not a good idea to rely on their presence. Stick to the natives if you want something nice on your plate to accompany the chips.

Summer time is when tope arrive off the storm beaches. If

these magnificent fish are your passion (and why shouldn't they be?) you can do no better than to attend Broughton Bay at the west end of Gower close to low water with a bag of whole herring or mackerel and heavy tackle.

One good specimen tope is likely to be the high spot of any angling holiday and Broughton Bay is the best place to catch it, although Pendine, Pembrey, Newgale and Dinas Dinlle beaches also produce some fine individuals. These vast beaches are spacious enough to get well away from the tourist crowds with a little backpacking. When the water temperature reaches a sensible level you can catch your own mackerel, with spinner or feathers, off the headlands or in fast moving channels between the mainland and offshore islands like those found at Mumbles Head or Burry Holmes in Gower and Ramsey Sound near St Davids.

The poorest time of the year for catching Welsh sea fish is undoubtedly between Christmas and April. Just as well – most anglers wouldn't contemplate taking a holiday at that time anyway. The rest of the winter can be quite exciting though. From late September the codling, cod and whiting are gradually feeding their way closer to the shore, eagerly searching for squidlug cocktails to sustain them. The pollack is still with us, too. Flounders, plaice and dabs are still pottering about the place, so are occasional heavy-duty bass. Some big bass will even spend all winter in favourable locations – solitary old-timers with nowhere else to go.

Bait is normally in reasonable supply though it does tend to be rather sparser the further west you go: if you want to dig your own, that is. There are a few tackle shops stocking fresh bait but they are a bit thin on the ground and unless you are there pretty early it will all be gone. It is best to take enough with you from your normal source of supply to last the first few days – at least until you get to know where to dig for it locally. And don't forget to take a garden fork!

Squid, sprats, herring and mackerel should be obtainable at the nearest wet-fish shop and you should keep a supply in your refrigerator as an emergency reserve.

All told, you should not experience much difficulty in digging for bait. Lugworms are to be found in the calmer parts of bays like Swansea and on the sides of estuaries like the Loughor and the Towy. Don't waste your time looking on the great storm beaches like Llangennith or Pembrey or you will have to spend all day to get enough to use. Deep digging for isolated specimens, if you can find them, is the only way. The heavy surf churns up the clean sand too much for them to make a living.

Ragworm, the small sort, is easily obtained in estuaries or close to sewage outlets but if you want to try king rag, forget it, unless you take your own from home. It just isn't found around the Welsh coast except in one small stretch west of Colwyn Bay, descendants, no doubt, from bait discarded after the many competitions held there. Razor fish can be found – just – if you take your container of salt to the right place at the very bottom of the tide, but don't rely too much on being able to get any or you will certainly be disappointed.

Now for the west Wales coast – a different proposition altogether. The broad sweep of Cardigan Bay right up to the Menai Strait does have its share of big beaches but they are all concentrated in the northern half. From St Davids Head up to Aberystwyth the only proper surf fishing is to be found in smallish coves and bays – and there are not many of those. Due to this dearth of sandy strand, the few bits which are available get packed with sun-worshippers and ball-kickers every day in summer when it's not actually raining; and even then elbow room can be at a premium.

It follows that nearly all the quietest fishing spots are from the rocks and usually have a rocky sea-bed. Many stands are difficult of access and some can be quite dangerous. Not to be recommended for the unfit! This is not a good part of the coastline for convenient sea angling unless you don't mind sharing the few bits of beach with hundreds of others or go there at antisocial times. Having said that, those prepared and able to put up with some inconvenience can reap good rewards with bass, using a spinner or float tackle. Pollack and mackerel too. Winter will provide good catches of whiting, cod, codling and pollack but there are very few spots where flat-fish can find their preferred environment.

There are plenty of slipways to launch a boat if the weather is right and good weather is essential for safe sailing in the Irish Sea. So is a proper navigational map of the coastline and a comprehensive store of lifesaving equipment. There are many dangerously rocky stretches on this coast with reefs sometimes extending a long way offshore and, as mentioned before, access is often difficult – sometimes impossible without a helicopter. Rescue of the foolish is often handicapped by the nature of this coast and tragedies *do* occur. So be cautious to the point of paranoia!

But don't allow this rather gloomy description to put you off visiting this part of Wales because it really is a beautiful area with lots of other things to do besides fish in the sea. Good fishing spots *can* be located with a little research and effort, so take your rods along by all means.

From Aberystwyth northwards there is a string of impressive beaches almost running into one another: Borth, Aberdovey, Tywyn, Fairbourne, Barmouth, Harlech, then west through Black Rock, Llanbedrog, Pwllheli, Aber-soch and the wild reaches of Hell's Mouth to Aberdaron.

Bass abound, so do all British flatties. There is some wonderful surf fishing here and access is generally easy. As in south Wales, these huge beaches allow undisturbed sport if you are prepared to walk a little way away from the main access points and car parks where most of the non-angling tourists gather.

The only severe problem on the west coast is bait. Lack of it, rather! There are a few places where it can be dug but it tends to congregate in small pockets and a lot of hard work has to be done to get enough for a day's fishing. Don't rely on tackle shops for a supply either. The best thing to do when holidaying around Cardigan Bay is to take fresh bait with you and set aside part of a day to travel to one of the places where it can be found, when your initial supply is running low or starting to pong. Appendix 2 at the end of this book may help you in locating the closest place.

Small ragworms can be found in the muddy parts of estuaries, but access is often not very easy because roads rarely get close enough to the water and private land invariably has to be crossed: not a good idea since the introduction of the Criminal

Justice (?) Act, 1994. There are a few harbours – Aberystwyth, Aberdovey, Barmouth and Aber-soch – where satisfactory amounts can be obtained. Otherwise it means scratching around and hoping for the best.

Lugworm is even less prolific. About the only halfway decent places are at the mouth of the Teifi at Poppit Sands near Cardigan, and that of the Dovey at Ynyslas or on Portmadoc sands. Aber-soch golf course sands provide a few, as well as razor fish at low tide, and there is a small patch on the west side of Aberdaron beach. That's about it, really. Soft crab can be picked from the rocks as usual, but the only other alternative is squid or fresh fish bait from a wet-fish shop – if you can find one. There aren't even many of *them*.

Now for the northern coast including the island of Anglesey. This is a much easier stretch to fish with a good mixture of long beaches, coves and rocks. It also includes the Menai Strait about which more later.

Starting at the tip of the Lleyn peninsula, with the exception of a few small coves and sheltered bays, the coastline is roughly similar to the southern part of Cardigan Bay; hard to fish, with a rough bottom and unruly mobs of famished, wandering crabs waiting to grab the bait before anything with fins gets a look-in. Incidentally, the rocky coasts of the Lleyn produce excellent lobsters and edible crabs. A lot of "potting" goes on here in the summer.

The situation changes abruptly at Dinas Dinlle south of Caernarfon, where a spectacular storm beach extends along several miles of low-lying ground at the base of the Snowdonia foothills. Arguably the best bass beach to be found in the country, it can sometimes be nearly impossible to hold the bottom in a strong west wind, and weed torn from the Lleyn rocks is capable of collecting on the line at an alarming rate during a making tide after a storm.

None of which detracts in the slightest from the good catches of big bass which can be made here from July to late autumn. The strong currents around the entrance to the Menai Strait at the northern end of the beach regularly propel shoals of bass, plaice and flounders up and down close to shore. The northern end of the beach is the best as well as being the quietest although deep water is close inshore the whole length at high tide.

A hop across the Strait at this point brings you on to the southeast corner of Anglesey. From here to Holyhead the land dips gently into the sea giving rise to wide stretches of sand interspersed with low, rocky peninsulas and islands. It can be a bit confusing to find your way around this coast but there are lots of good places to cast a line and a nice bag of fish shouldn't be too hard to collect. A bonus is the magnificent backdrop of Snowdon and its guardian colleagues dominating the skyline on a clear day. It doesn't really matter if you don't catch anything among such scenery as this. Still, the fish are there – it's up to you to persuade them to come ashore.

From Holyhead across the top of the island to the northern entrance of the Menai Strait, the land is much higher and great cliffs plunge straight into the sea between the holiday beaches. More people tend to gravitate to this sector but it shouldn't be too hard to find a relatively peaceful spot, especially if you are prepared to do a bit of exploring before committing yourself.

Much of Anglesey's coastline is a haven for dogfish. Indeed, the catching of them is a local industry. Lines are used but the dogfish seem to be unable to distinguish a commercial hook from one belonging to a solitary angler. Whatever else you catch around Anglesey's shores you can always be sure of a dogfish in the bag.

The Menai Strait is in a class of its own when it comes to quality of fish, so much so, that in 1985 it was designated the first Marine Nature Reserve in Britain by the Nature Conservancy Council. The trouble is, it's so difficult to fish for most of its length. Currents are not so much strong as terrifyingly powerful. When the flow is running fast during the spring tides it's like looking at a very big river compressed into a narrow gorge in spate conditions. The 84 minute difference in tides at either end of the 20 mile (32 km) waterway can often produce a race in excess of 8 knots.

There are several good boating clubs in the area and the boating angler is strongly urged to obtain proper advice from one of them about local hazards before ever attempting to sail in these waters for the first time, particularly in the vicinity of the two bridges near the northern end. When using a boat for fishing around here or in the northern sector of Anglesey make sure your engine is in tip-top condition and has enough guts to get you out of trouble. The currents can be unexpectedly strong around headlands and over shallows. Take enough fuel and while you're at it check the integrity of your life-saving gear as any sensible boater should – and hope you never need to use it.

Back to the Menai fish! Bass everywhere, following the strong currents, searching for tasty crabs over the rocky bottom and ragworm in the calmer reaches. Flat-fish in any quantity are mostly found at either end of the Strait due to the scarcity of convenient sandy areas, but where they are found they are in abundance. Tope are regular visitors to the shifting sandbanks of the southern approaches and cruise along the waterway with the current. Very big conger eels patrol the rocky hollows of the middle Strait. Try these with a large whole mackerel or herring; you have a good chance if the crabs are torpid. There are many muddy lagoons where mullet pursue their laid-back feeding habits. Mullet also congregate in large numbers and size around the weedy walls of the harbour at Port Dinorwic. In winter, codling, cod, whiting and pollack are present in great amounts.

All of which combines to make the area of the Menai Strait one of the best for fishing in the British Isles. But there's always a down side, isn't there? What is it? Access, that's what! Both banks are notoriously difficult to approach and vehicle parking is limited to just a few places within easy reach of the waterside. As well as being difficult of approach it is also hard to move from your initial stand as the gully sides are steep and rocky. Still, the holiday angler does have a choice of places to which he can go without too much of a problem, mostly on the Anglesey side.

Starting from the north end there is the sinisterly-named Gallows Point at Beaumaris, a good stand for bass and flatties at low tide. A bit to the right, on the mainland, you will see Bangor Pier, highly recommended if you are prepared to share it with day trippers. Further south, on the Anglesey side, it is worth trying a selection of muddy lagoons for flounders or mullet. Around the base of Telford's suspension bridge you will find several easy stands from which deep water can be plumbed – but the bottom is not hook or weight-friendly, currents are fierce and the crabs are merciless.

Harlech Beach. Sand, surf, bass and flatties; what more do you want?

The next easy access point is the harbour at Port Dinorwic but parking is at a premium here in the main tourist season. On the same shore there are only a couple of access points until you get south of Caernarfon. A marine drive runs alongside the water's edge here and the fishing is good even though the bottom is rotten, acres of weedy stones being the norm. Nevertheless there are some clear spaces to be found if you seek them out at low tide. Crabs are again a severe problem.

On the opposite side of the Strait there are several good stands from the Mermaid south over a sandy bottom. This is where you should try for a tope, but be very careful not to become encircled by an incoming tide on one of the sandbanks. The Menai Strait is not kind to the unwary. Right at the bottom is Abermenai Point, an excellent fishing stand, Unfortunately, like all good things in life, it is hard to get at, a long walk of more than two miles (3.2 km) over soft sand being the only way, so those with coronary problems had better not try it. Leave this area to the young 'uns or those who have something to prove.

Heading east from the Menai Strait, the first stretch of beach you come to is the vast expanse of sand known as Traeth Lafan. Keep well away from here! The tide goes out so far it has to return as fast as you can run in order to stick to its schedule. The eastern end is OK, though, and holds plenty of flatfish – even bass when the surf is up.

In fact, bass can be caught as far east as Prestatyn but beyond here they fizzle out and are replaced with species preferring a muddy bottom such as flounders, whiting and dabs. This coastline is heavily exploited by the tourist trade and beach nets, yet it can still be quite easy to locate a place to fish and there are plenty of fish to catch, too. Shrimpers can often reap a bountiful harvest between Conway and Prestatyn.

Fresh bait is easy to find and dig for yourself. Lug are in abundance at the mouths of rivers along with rag, cockles and mussels. There are also many fair-sized towns where other baits may be purchased.

As far as the boating angler is concerned, usable slipways are not as numerous as one would like, so check on their availability close to where you are staying.

Chapter 8

Obtaining Permits

Let the Englishman have what he's after,
A wild-running brookful of crystal water
Through some dear glen.

Goronwy Owen   1723-1769

SEVERAL YEARS AGO a Welsh angler decided to have a day's fishing on a river he had never tried before. Many times he had travelled on the road running alongside, sometimes stopping to watch trout rising in the long, clear pools separated by rippling, pebbly runs and promised himself a treat one day.

The weekend weather forecast predicted perfect conditions and just to refresh his memory the angler once more read the entry on this particular stretch in a "Where to fish" booklet. Apparently there was more than two miles (3.2 km) of both banks controlled by the local club. Salmon, sea-trout and trout were in residence, although the angler's prime interest was brown trout likely to be tempted by a dry fly.

The character of the water was particularly suitable for this discipline, much of it being of a chalk-stream nature. An address was given where permits could be obtained but no prices were mentioned. No problem! The outing could always be altered if the tickets were too expensive but this was very unlikely. A treat's a treat, after all.

The river happened to be at the other end of Wales. An early start would be needed to travel the 150 miles (241 kms) to the water. The angler and his colleague arrived at about midday and turned off the main road to the village bridge in order to have a look at the prospects. The shop which dispensed permits had been spotted close to the junction.

Clear, sparkling water flowed under the bridge. Streamers of clean, healthy weed waved in the current and flies danced in clouds over the water and around the bushes. There was hardly any rubbish on the bottom; an unusual state of affairs near a road bridge. Several trout of good size swayed in the gaps between the water weed; many small, a couple about a pound (454 grams) in weight and one clonker which must have been close to two pounds (907 grams). The prognosis looked good and a pleasant day was envisaged.

A short walk from the bridge brought the angler back to the shop. Entering, he waited while a couple of customers were served then asked for two permits to fish for the day. The shopkeeper was very apologetic but he was afraid he could not oblige. When asked the reason why, he demurred and it needed a bit of interrogation to get the facts out of him

Apparently, in spite of the entry in the "Where to fish" book, a copy of which was produced in evidence, only people living or staying in the village were entitled to purchase permits and he was sorry, a 300 mile (482 km) round trip notwithstanding, he could not issue a permit and that was that. "Take it up with the author!" he suggested.

The angler left the shop, angry and disillusioned, and immediately travelled a bit further to another river where day tickets were available. A very pleasant day's fishing was had but this did not go very far to disperse the keen sense of disappointment at what had happened.

Many more mistakes were found in this particular booklet, so many, in fact, that it was soon discarded in favour of speaking to anglers on the river and asking them for local advice.

Now it is not easy to compile a "Where to fish" book and a little reflection will show why. In the example given above, if day tickets were handed out to everyone who wanted to fish that particular river there would be standing-room only along both banks. It is the only club-controlled stretch on that river as well as being in the heart of the most visited tourist area in Wales. The locals wouldn't get a look-in! They cannot be blamed for wishing to preserve their water against hordes of visiting anglers.

None of which excuses the fact that such a glaring omission from the book of the true facts must have caused many visiting anglers to have a wasted day, especially those not familiar with the area. It can't have been much fun for the shopkeeper either. It had provoked a negative perception of Welsh hospitality – and also quite a false one. The fault lies squarely with the book and the important information it left out.

Another example. The same angler had often stayed at a cottage near a famous salmon river. One year he checked with the local permit distributor and was given the cost of a weekly ticket. Reasonably priced – fine! On the strength of this he booked the cottage again for a week in September when the main run of salmon would be in full swing. When he arrived in September, he immediately went to the same distributor to buy a weekly ticket, only to be told that they were not issued after the last day of August. He had not been told this earlier in the year and consequently had to spend that week fishing on other rivers much further afield instead of just walking down the road as he had anticipated.

To a holiday angler taking his first fishing outing in Wales this kind of thing can be a decided turn-off; but what can he do to avoid such disappointments?

It's not easy! But there is a way.

First, in spite of what has previously been said about "Where to fish" books, borrow or buy one for the area you are visiting. No compiler of such a book can possibly keep up with all the differing rules, conditions and restrictions for all the clubs in Wales every year and not include some mistakes and outdated information. Rules are normally added to or changed at the club's annual general meeting without informing the book's author. Bear one thing in mind; whatever information is given, that information will very likely be correct up to a point.

Most often this point will be the quotation of the price of the tickets (where given). Always expect the actual price to be higher than that shown in the book. Ticket prices have a habit of rising each year and those given in the book may be based upon the previous year's prices – or even the year before that. Sometimes such information is many years out of date. Some experiences of the author may usefully be mentioned at this point.

On one occasion, expecting a day ticket to be £2 (as advised in the book), a visit to the distributor resulted in £5 being paid to avoid both a long, wasted trip and an unpleasant scene. This, in spite of the fact that the sum of £2 was printed on the ticket together with the current year of issue. The £2 had been crossed out with a biro and £5 written alongside. It was noticed that the next ticket in the book had not been altered in the same way, and it was darkly suspected that the shopkeeper had altered the amount himself and pocketed the difference. Watch out for this practice!

Another time, day tickets had been regularly taken out on a particularly lovely river for fifteen years. On the first trip to this river early one season, the first thing noticed was that the ownership of the shop which issued the tickets had changed. On asking for a day ticket as usual, the answer was received that none were available. A brief chat on the phone with the estate office brought forth the information that the issue of tickets had ceased six years previously. This meant that for six years anyone who purchased a ticket was technically poaching, in spite of paying the required amount. The estate office never received any of the revenue. Fortunately they allowed the author to fish free of charge on this occasion so there was a happy ending in this case at least.

The vast majority of ticket distributors are honest, thank goodness! But not all are anglers themselves and this can also give rise to a whole lot of misunderstandings, not least of which are concerned with where the permit allows you to fish. Where are the boundaries? What are the club rules?

We shall take these in turn.

The usual day or weekly ticket will be a small slip of paper with the date of issue and the name of the club written on it, together with a couple of lines where the purchasing angler writes his name and address. Rarely will there be any precise guide to the waters you are allowed to fish, and questions on this subject asked of the distributor are often answered in vague terms. Just as confusing is the ticket which gives a brief written description of the waters available. They always assume a minute knowledge of local place names, boundaries described by the name of a pool, the lands of a farm or obscure landmarks, none of which can be located on a large scale map no matter how thoroughly it is studied.

Worse still is a description something like "from. . . to. . . except for a couple of small stretches under private ownership" or "with certain exceptions". This is a terrible position in which to put a visiting angler who has paid his cash in good faith into the club's coffers only to be told he will have to find out whether he is trespassing or not at his own risk. And we all know how proprietorial some riparian owners can be, don't we?

The holiday angler new to the area will often have to guess where his permit allows him to fish without incurring the wrath of other riparian owners, many of whom are fed up to the back teeth with innocent anglers fishing where they have no right to be. You would be surprised how often this situation arises and the fault can be placed wholly at the door of angling clubs who display an amazingly casual attitude to the rights and welfare of others. The trouble is that an angler caught fishing where he is not supposed to be, even if his permit did not tell him so, can be hauled up before the beak on a poaching charge. This can be enough to blight any holiday.

One can, of course, imagine the reaction of the same club if an angler is caught fishing on its water innocently believing he is entitled to do so. The club will come down on him like the proverbial ton of something and totally ignore the fact that they are putting their own customers in the same position.

A few clubs – a very few – go to the trouble of printing a map of their waters. This is especially useful when the club's waters are scattered around several rivers in short stretches. Unfortunately such maps are rarely up to date and once more use obscure (to the visiting angler) names to designate the boundaries. Some are obvious, a road or rail bridge, for example, while others can only be recognized by the locals. Access points to the water are not often shown where the river is at some distance from a road and this can lead to the holiday angler having to cross fields and ditches without really knowing whether he is trespassing. To top it all, even when a map is available some clubs actually levy a charge for a copy.

Admittedly the club may have to pay a small sum to have a map copied. However, it is difficult to defend a charge of £1 for a copy of a map (as more than one club does) when everyone knows it only costs 10p at present to use the photocopier in the local library. Such parsimonious practices create a very poor impression. No! More than that. It's a rip-off which should be discontinued forthwith. An unambiguous map and a copy of the rules should automatically be issued with every permit to protect the purchaser from inadvertently getting into trouble, and any costs for their publication absorbed in the price of the ticket. Disclaimers printed on the ticket may be legally valid but they are morally and ethically indefensible. Club secretaries, please note!

Even when the poor, abused angler reaches what he thinks is the boundary of the club's water he can still be mistaken. Nearly all clubs erect boards at the end of their stretches but very few believe in ensuring their continued legibility after a few years of rain and wind have taken their toll of the paintwork. How often have you seen a rectangle of board nailed to a tree with absolutely nothing written thereon? All too common, regrettably, and which side of the notice belongs to the club, anyway? This is not often clear.

Club rules? Rarely are any but the most important displayed

A nice, open stretch of the River Elan headwaters just above the famous Elan Valley reservoirs in mid-Wales. Stealth and long casts are required to tempt the wary residents.

on the ticket. More often there is simply a note to the effect that there *are* other rules but they are either contained in a separate booklet or included as part of the club's constitution. A request for a copy of the same will inevitably elicit a blank stare or a suggestion that the inquirer contact the club secretary, none of which helps in the slightest.

Rules are important. They help to manage local fishing and ensure that anglers don't tread on anyone's toes. Unless you know what the rules are, you run the risk of falling foul of one of them and having your permit revoked. Not very fair when you couldn't get a copy of them in the first place, is it?

Some clubs will not allow dogs to accompany anglers on the water. Some place restrictions on certain pools, even only allowing you to fish on certain days of the week, at certain times of day and only then if the water is above or below a certain height. On this last point, regulations which are activated by a certain water height (to allow spinning for migratory fish, for instance) very rarely state where to find the marker against which this criterion has to be measured. Again the visiting angler must guess – if he manages to find out about the rule in the first place, that is.

Sometimes an angler must stop fishing in a pool after a certain time if another angler indicates he wishes to fish the same pool. There may be restrictions on what type of tackle is permitted – no fixed-spool reels allowed for spinning, for instance – or a minimum size of spinner before a certain date.

All these rules are important, evolved over the years for good reasons. But if you can't get a copy of them. . . !

One last criticism before finishing with the club-bashing:

the question of being able to get along the river banks to fish the whole stretch.

Not every angler is in the prime of life. A great many suffer from handicaps of one sort or another – an ageing heart, rapidly getting out of puff, stiffness in the limbs or other ailments which make it rather difficult to get around with ease. The older one gets the more likely one is to be suffering from some infirmity which can make a small obstruction assume the proportions of a major obstacle.

We've all met them. The barbed wire fence too high to climb over which extends right down the bank to a deep, unwadeable pool; the broken stile which wobbles frighteningly when any weight is placed on the slippery, rotting cross-piece; the steep muddy track plunging straight down the bank into the water ; or the gap at the side of a road bridge only a skeleton can squeeze through giving immediate access to a dive straight down to the bone-breaking rocks below without any footholds.

Hazards like these are capable of greatly restricting the available water which even an only slightly handicapped angler can get to, which is a bit much when he is expected to pay the same price for a permit as a younger and fitter person who is able to fish all the water – including that a long way from any access.

Some clubs are aware of this and go to a lot of trouble to alleviate the situation. One in particular, in north-west Wales, has a magnificent track record in this regard. Not only are well-maintained stiles and gates put at nearly every obstacle, or close by, but the association has even negotiated parking privileges in the most heavily fished areas close to the river and access has been made easy for all but the most severely disabled of anglers. What a pity this attitude is not universal.

Unfortunately such is not the case. All too often the luckless angler has to struggle through thick undergrowth, snagging his expensive waders on rusty barbed wire, negotiating seemingly bottomless mud holes or risking his life trying to get down to the river over a precipitous bridge parapet. Anyone over middle age can have a terrible time just getting to the water. If he does manage to do so and fishes up the first meadow he will often find his way then barred by an impenetrable fence and will only be able to continue by entering the water which can be a bit dangerous if the river is coloured or in spate.

All clubs which distribute permits must understand that although there is no legal requirement to provide safe access, they do have a moral responsibility over and above simply taking out a form of public liability insurance. To take somebody's money and then effectively deny him the enjoyment of the water as is the case with a significant number of handicapped individuals is not only wrong but also suggests a neglect of river management in other respects, i.e. a sloppy and disinterested attitude.

Although a large number of clubs do provide limited means to overcome natural obstructions, there are many which do nothing at all. Any holiday angler who meets with such neglect should write a letter of complaint to the secretary of the club. This may help in producing benefits for all concerned, not least to the club itself.

The responsibility for minimising obstacles to a worry-free day of fishing is mostly down to the club issuing the ticket.

Hardly any bother to do so to an acceptable measure. It must be said, in mitigation, that this attitude is not confined to Welsh waters. Many English, Scottish and Irish angling associations are guilty of the same practices. The onus is therefore upon you, the holiday angler, to sort things out before you actually set out in order to avoid any disappointments.

There is one easy way to do it.

Having bought your "Where to fish" book, study the entries in the vicinity of the area you would prefer to visit before booking the holiday. There will probably be several clubs from which to choose and almost certainly the names and phone number of the club secretary or local permit distributor. Any "Where to fish" book which does not include this information is not worth purchasing.

Now make a list of the questions to which you want answers. A suggested selection is as follows and you may wish to add some of your own.

➤ First ask whether they issue day, week or monthly tickets during the time you are visiting even if you are not staying in the immediate vicinity.

➤ Then request the rates.

➤ If you do not have the appropriate rod licence for your anticipated form of fishing ask whether the distributor can supply one and if not, the nearest place you can purchase one.

Enquire whether an accurate map of the waters and a comprehensive list of club rules is available.

Ascertain whether there are restrictions about when a ticket can be purchased, such as the local early closing day, or if the distributor shuts up shop at other times.

If you have any infirmities, ask if the water is suitable for you; whether it is in a dangerous gorge or requires a lot of deep wading on slippery bare rock; if stiles are provided to cross fences, etc.

Ask if there are severe restrictions on the tackle allowed to be used. e.g. fly only, etc.

Finally thank the person contacted by phone or letter for their time and advice, not forgetting to ask if you may contact them again if you meet with any difficulties. They will invariably be pleased to agree.

Armed with this information you will be able to reduce enormously the frustration and confusion which can be encountered when fishing unknown waters. At the very least it will enable you to know how much the club values the well-being of its paying guests and at best it should completely avoid spoiling what should be an extremely enjoyable interlude on Welsh waters.

Chapter 9

Where To Stay

The inns will furnish every want and wish,
For there he'll find good flesh, good fowl, good fish;
And those who on crimp salmon wish to feast.

Edward Davies   1718-1789

SO YOU'VE DECIDED which part of Wales you would like to visit, checked up on the local fishing as well as you can and contacted the permit distributor to find out if there is anything you should know about to avoid problems. So far all is well. Now what?

The only thing left is to decide where to stay. What alternatives does Wales have to offer, and what are their advantages and limitations?

There are many different choices to suit all pockets, except perhaps those of the entirely destitute, and even then there are plenty of nice woods and hedgerows under which to shelter. Camping under canvas, caravanning, chalets, bed and breakfast, hotels or guest-houses, farm accommodation, self-catering cottages or relatives who live in Wales – all are suitable.

Working on the assumption that those who stay with relatives will be familiar with their surroundings, let us investigate the pros and cons of the other types of shelter.

You've got a caravan or dormobile, eh? That's nice. With either of those you have one enormous advantage over those who choose any other form of accommodation – speedy mobility. You can stay more or less where you wish and if the fishing at your first location does not live up to expectations you can move on to another, even alternate between the fleshpots of the coast (to keep the family quiet) and the peace of the mountains if you like. Compromise can be an essential ingredient for domestic harmony.

There are enormous numbers of sites at which to stay, mostly on the coast but a more than adequate number inland too. Sea angling caravanners need only check their caravan site guide to discover the nearest location to where they wish to pursue their sport. All it takes is a phone call to confirm a pitch and book it on the spot. While you are on the phone it is advisable to ask whether there is direct access to the beach and how far away it is. You could find yourself perched on the top of a high cliff with a three mile (5 km) trip to the nearest beach access. Even if there is some sort of a path down the cliff it may be rather difficult climbing back up without assistance to help carry a large catch of bass or plaice.

People have differing ideas about what constitutes the perfect caravan site; some like a club room or bar – some don't, for instance. Whatever your preferences, try to find out about everything which will affect your fishing before you commit yourself and book a pitch. It could save a lot of frustration later on. A good holiday may still be enjoyed but the fishing will suffer.

As mentioned before, mobility is the primary purpose of a

mobile home so there is no good reason why you should stay in one location. Indeed, you improve your chances of finding a fishing spot which suits you but it is not such a good idea to try and cover too much territory in one go. Split Wales up into about four manageable sections and try one on each visit. This will enable you to cover a particular area of the country reasonably thoroughly, instead of a lot of country superficially.

Suggested areas would be the north and south coastal strips with the central portion split into two.

The south Wales holiday strip properly begins at Swansea and extends westwards although there are some very pleasant sites to be found further east, including the popular holiday centres of Barry Island and Porth-cawl. West of Swansea is the Gower peninsular, the first area of outstanding natural beauty to be so designated, and deservedly so. Since its appointment it has managed to retain most of its attraction in spite of the pressures placed upon its natural resources by an increasingly greedy and destructive society. Several active organizations in the area are continually striving to keep it that way, with some success.

Further west, with the exception of the St Ishmael's holiday camp near Kidwelly (an excellent base for the sea angler), there is not much choice until Pendine is reached. From here on there are plenty of sites to suit all tastes, both within walking distance of the beach and up the valleys towards the mountains.

The north Wales coastal holiday strip properly starts at Prestatyn and stretches all the way to, and through, Anglesey. As a general rule the further west you go the more likely you are to find smaller and quieter sites in more scenic surroundings.

Heading inland from the northern coast and away from the A55 expressway, the mountains dominate everything. Nearly all the western part is included in the Snowdonia National Park and as a result the proliferation of large, sprawling caravan parks is strictly limited and controlled for a variety of very good reasons. The coastal strip has the majority but there are a large number of smaller sites well inland in narrow valleys away from the main roads. These should be the first choice of the game angler because most of them are close to a river, stream or lake – many are right alongside one – and the fishing rights are often owned by the site owners, many of whom are farmers.

Farmers can apply to the local authority for a planning licence allowing them the right to use one or more of their fields for touring caravans – a useful source of income to the hard-pressed hill farm after the sheep have been dispersed to the high mountain pastures in summer. Many of these temporary sites afford spectacular views of the surroundings and are far from the crowds.

Three, five, eight or more caravans may be allowed depending upon the impact on the environment as assessed by the local authority; they don't want their territories littered with small gaggles of mobile homes all over the place, after all. Nobody can dispute the detrimental effect this type of development could have on the surroundings. Without sensitive regulation it can ruin the very tranquillity and beauty which visitors come to enjoy.

Even if the right to fish is not offered on site it is worth asking the landowner about it. He may be renting the fishing rights to a club which has more water elsewhere, even on another river, and the site owner would at least be able to give you some information on the local picture.

Prior knowledge about these smaller inland sites is essential if you are to avoid the exasperation of travelling round and round trying to find a suitable place to stay. Most of them are very small – only spaces for up to a couple of dozen vans – and some are so well hidden among the crags and trees that it is unlikely you will ever stumble upon them by accident. Consult a site directory such as that published by the Caravan Club and this will also provide the assurance that the site has at least

The Wye. A nice run alongside the park in Builth Wells.

been inspected and found not to be wanting in any significant regard.

This part of Wales should be assumed to end roughly along the route of the A44 eastwards from Aberystwyth. South of this road the situation changes somewhat. Along the coast of Cardigan Bay good sites are in abundance, but inland there is a distinct shortage, and they become somewhat harder to find the further east you go. This is not to say they are rare but they are certainly spread further apart than in the rest of Wales.

Unless you consult the site directory the best places for mobile home owners to look are close to the headwaters of the major rivers like the Teifi, Aeron, Cothi or Tawe. These hill farms have the benefit of the best scenery as well as being the hardest to make a living out of solely by farming; the farmers are therefore more likely to seek extra income by accommodating tourists.

But you may not have a mobile home, in which case renting a chalet or static caravan permanently stationed on a site may fit your requirements. There are many ways of finding out where such places are available: small ads in the local paper, glossy brochures from the big operators by post or in the travel agents, word of mouth from friends who have been there, or by reference to caravan site directories often available at the local reference library. If you can't get a recommendation from a friend, perhaps the best way to find a suitable location is to use one of the directories. You know they will be up to scratch and a phone number is always given. Make a list of your choices and work through it by phone until you find one which can accommodate you on your preferred dates.

A lot of these chalets and static caravans are owned by individuals who pay the landowner a leasehold fee. Under these circumstances the site owner may only be able to give you the phone number or address of the accommodation owner, and suggest you contact them directly to make booking arrangements. Most site owners keep a list of those prepared to let their premises. On the other hand, the site manager sometimes does the booking arrangements on behalf of the owners and collects a small fee for doing so. In this case you can organize things immediately.

It is extremely rare to find a static caravan or chalet which is in a poor state. Especially in Wales! In the unthinkable event of your being unlucky, react! Please! The Tourist Board and the local authority will be very interested – that's their job – but don't go grizzling to them until after you have consulted the site manager and/or the owner. Mistakes *can* happen.

You can expect a very good standard on Welsh sites. Even elderly static caravans can be like little palaces inside with everything up to date and in first class order. It is up to you to help keep things that way, so leave the place as you would expect to find it!

Of course you have to be a socially compatible and gregarious type to habitually take your holidays on a permanent site. Not all of us are. Not all of us want to do our fishing within the confines of a field full of people, putting up with them, their dogs or their wretched offspring throwing stones, swimming, walking along the bank and disturbing the fish, watching you for hours on end wondering whether you will ever catch anything. No, not everyone's cup of tea.

Perhaps you would rather stay at a hotel or guest-house instead? The holiday angler would do well to consider this type of lodging especially if he is going solo. The seaside towns would not generally be suitable nor, for that matter, the centres of most of the inland towns, if only for the fact that muddy clothing and smelly bait do not cohabit well with posh environs or invite the approval of houseproud landladies.

With all due respect to those admirable proprietors who invariably provide cheap, clean and comfortable lodgings, it is far better for the holiday angler to find room at one of the hostelries which specialize in field and sporting pursuits and are therefore familiar with the eccentricities and shortcomings of those who do the pursuing.

Now here is a strange fact about Welsh angling hotels. Compared to the other game fishing areas in the UK there are very few of them, it would seem. They are not often advertised. This, in a land full of good game rivers and dotted with lakes of all sizes. Have a look in the hotel accommodation offered in one of the glossy game fishing magazines early in the year. It is likely there will be several pages devoted to sporting hostelries in Scotland, Ireland and the West Country but if there is as much as half a page referring to Wales it will be unusual.

Whatever the true reason for this it behoves the holiday angler, desirous of spending a relaxing week or so in one of the Welsh fishing hotels, to book well in advance.

Mostly located well out in the countryside, these hostelries are not quite as numerous as they once were. They come in all shapes: sometimes modern, brash and out of place in their surroundings, but more often, traditional, even old-fashioned in appearance and blending into the countryside as if organically grown there. These latter hostelries are every bit as comfortable and clean as their modern equivalents and exude a cosy atmosphere of welcome and conviviality most people would associate with another age.

In days gone by, before foreign destinations became within reach of most working folk, the annual couple of weeks of relaxation would normally have been spent in a hotel or guest-house at a British seaside resort. This is how those imposing lines of promenade buildings became established in the first place. But away from the coast many hotels were built around or near springs or wells reputed to have beneficial medical effects, physical ones, that is. Little is known of the mental effects contracted from these wells in areas of heavy metal deposits, and as many of these spa hotels were of the temperance persuasion even the benediction of alcohol was not available to counteract any damage done by taking the waters.

And there is one other benefit of staying at a sporting hotel – being able to have a drink at the end of a pleasant day's fishing without having to worry about the breathalyser. There may be a few temperance hotels still in existence but most have removed the shackles of dogma and cater for their guests in the manner to be expected of a modern hotel. Sitting in the bar, clutching a glass you seem unable to empty, in the convivial company of other anglers and locals, yarning about fishing experiences of the past and trying to think up plausible excuses for not catching much that day – this setting is one of the most relaxing pastimes to be found anywhere.

Several hostelries advertise themselves as field-sport-oriented without having any sporting rights of their own to offer as part of the package. Unless they are very close to (within easy walking distance of) a river or lake to which you will definitely be able to gain access, these are to be avoided. Any sporting hotel worthy of the description will have fishing rights of its own, or concessions on adjoining water. In most cases (not all) there will be an extra charge for the fishing but it must be remembered that not everybody who stays there will want to fish so why should they be expected to subsidize those who do?

Have a look at the advertisements in the game fishing magazines for a selection of hotels with fishing attached. The ubiquitous "Where to fish" books will often mention other places, usually those which also offer day tickets to non-residential anglers. If you want to stay at one of these just phone up and make a provisional booking, at the same time asking whether you can expect relatively undisturbed fishing; i.e. is there a limit on tickets issued to non-residents or is it likely to be elbow to elbow all along the stretch?

Most of the fishing hotels are on the banks of the big rivers, the Wye and certain tributaries, the Clwyd, Teifi, Dee, Usk and the like. A few of the lakes are blessed with comfortable hostelries, too; Lake Vyrnwy and Tal-y-llyn can be cited as notable examples. Some are cheap, others are horrendously expensive. Remember, you pay for what is available, but you don't always get what you pay for if you spend most of your time in the bar. This is not a profitable method of catching fish.

A list of many of the Welsh hotels offering fishing in their tariffs is displayed in Appendix 1 at the end of this volume.

Most will provide packed meals and many can cater for night fishing by arrangement.

Hotels too expensive for you? Well perhaps we can cut the cost a bit without losing most of the benefits. On the lesser streams, as well as the occasional hotel with water to offer, there is another sort of accommodation which is well worth considering – the farmhouse providing bed and breakfast. Some will offer full board, of course, and they can be found on the larger rivers as well.

It is not so easy to find a place to stay if this sort of fishing holiday is required. Unless you are lucky enough to spot a small-ad or are told where to go by someone else, it may be better to look around for such a place on your initial Welsh angling holiday. Pick the river you wish to try and travel the roads and lanes running alongside looking out for a sign at one of the farm entrances offering accommodation. All you have to do then is knock on the door and make enquiries. Ask the price, naturally, then enquire whether there is any fishing to be enjoyed in the river running through the land owned by the farm or any other farm they may own. If there is, write down their address and phone number and arrange to contact them when you know the date you will next have some leave. There may be several other farms offering accommodation on the same river. Get details from these as well and take your pick.

And not only farmhouses either. All through the country you can find private houses where you can rent a comfortable room on a bed and breakfast basis. Many will be happy to provide full board if asked. A disadvantage is that they will rarely have any fishing of their own.

A further development of this type of accommodation is the self-catering holiday cottage, surely the most versatile of all. Wales has a very large number of these, in spite of rabid opposition from a few extreme nationalist organizations. There is only one real disadvantage – you will have to cook and clean for yourself instead of having it done for you – but this isn't any different from renting a caravan, is it?

Just consider the advantages instead. Most are well out in the country away from other people and among the fields and small lanes. Many will allow fishing in the rivers running through adjoining land and this is often included in the deal at no extra charge. Pets can be taken with you, sometimes free or at an extra charge, although this concession is becoming rarer for some reason. It is true that restrictions are becoming more common year by year. Children are not allowed in some places and smoking is banned in others. One day we may find a place which specifies a compulsory smoking rule in retaliation.

Still, most are flexible in their rules and you have the choice of not bothering with those you consider unacceptable. You are able to come and go as you please, have the freedom of any adjoining land, and don't have to see anyone if you don't want to. It is a perfect way to really hide away for a week or two.

Catalogues are available from several large self-catering agents. A list of some known to the author is given in Appendix 4. There are many smaller local agents too.

Most will print a picture of the premises offered and this will enable you to judge whether the surroundings are what you want. The number of bedrooms, domestic facilities and other inclusions such as fishing, shooting, use of a swimming pool or suitability for the disabled will be described in the text as well as any difficulties like vehicle accessibility or terrible TV reception – not an uncommon situation among the high mountains.

The river or lake fishing offered with some of these holiday cottages can be quite extensive and of excellent quality. You may possibly have to share the water with members of a club or syndicate who pay a rental to the farmer but this is rarely a disadvantage. Meeting one of the locals on the bank is often the passport to discovering a wealth of knowledge about the local fishing prospects and you also have the advantage of being

Long casting in a classic end-of-pool glide on the Dee downstream of Bala with grayling in mind.

able to fish any time of the day or night.

Yes, a self-catering holiday with fishing attached is just about the best of all worlds for the holiday angler. The family will love it but make sure the housekeeping is shared out between everyone or it won't be such a good time for your wife. Her cooperation is essential if you wish to do the same thing again.

One other type of holiday must be mentioned for the sake of comprehensiveness – camping. Whether you do it by car and trailer, motor cycle, pedal cycle or hitch-hiking, it can be a wonderfully free and easy way of getting around if the weather is right. Most caravan sites cater for campers, so do many farms, and if all else fails there are always the eternal mountains on which to find a sheltered spot.

Remember that Wales has a heck of a lot of steep hills so backpacking and cycling are only really recommended for the fit, active and hairy-chested. Advantages: absolute freedom to go to places a car will never reach; camping on sites far away from other human beings; keeping fit (or catching pneumonia); the chance to alter timetables and routes on a whim, to do what you want or do nothing except meditate.

Disadvantages: you can only take what you can carry so fishing tackle will have to be pared to a basic minimum. A strict regime must be followed in the matter of proper camping practice and eating times; biting insects must be accepted as normal and bad weather (never forget the Welsh reputation for rain) must be endured *in situ*. Cycling and hiking don't have a lot going for them if you want to do a lot of fishing but they are great ways – probably the best (and cheapest) – of getting to know the ins and outs of a sector of countryside you intend visiting again one day.

Brightly-coloured tents are often discovered by anglers who are toiling along a river bank, and it is frequently possible to do some sort of a deal with their occupants. Billy-cans of hot, sweet tea or coffee have frequently been exchanged for a couple of fat trout fresh from the stream to the benefit of both parties

Whatever sort of accommodation you decide upon, book in plenty of time or you may find your choices rather restricted. Wales is a popular venue for tourists and holidaymakers of all sorts and most of the best places are booked up well in advance.

It would be such a horrible shame if all you could get was the offer of a package holiday abroad – at double the price and never a fish in sight!

Chapter 10

Angling Etiquette

And let the humble artisan enjoy
The angler's gentle art, without annoy.

Richard Hall   1817 – 1866

SOME OF TODAY'S favourite grumbles have remained unchanged since the human race was first invented. "The world's going to the dogs. People just don't care any more. All they seem to do is rush, rush, rush without any consideration for others. Grab all and give nothing, that's them!" And so on, and so on.

A lot of truth in such sentiments you may think, and you are not alone by any means. Every other generation has said the same things with equal fervour and justification. Selfishness, the natural product of unbridled competition, permeates everything and everywhere. The work environment can be one of the worst. The rats racing on the shop floor have always been engaged in a pitched battle with the snake-pit of Head Office and there is no reason to expect it will ever be any different. Going on holiday is a good way of escaping, albeit only temporarily, from this suffocating and stressful maelstrom.

So there you are, sitting quietly on the river bank under a cool tree at the tail end of a beautiful pool waiting for a fish to thrust muscular shoulders above the surface in pursuit of a fly, and what happens? With a tinkling of happy laughter, a rush of running feet and a clatter of plastic utensils, along comes Joe and Jane Public with their brood of young thugs to enjoy a picnic right where you want to fish.

You are spotted. Up comes Joe with the inevitable "Caught any yet?" Glaring eyes and the gnash of grinding teeth are ignored. Joe fondly watches his foul offspring gather handfuls of stones and throw them in the run under the trees where the best fish always lie; the ones you had been waiting for. A large dog plunges in after the stones. Waves lash the banks dislodging lumps of clay which discolour the water downstream. Erosion and entropy are accelerated.

The unfortunate angler can do nothing to retrieve the situation. Other than starting a fight to the death, his only recourse is to shuffle off up the bank, growling under his breath, to another pool away from the spoilers.

Would you behave like Joe and his tribe? Of course not. No true anglers would display such discourtesy.

Or would they?

If any logo were to be adopted by the fishing fraternity it should read something like "Always be courteous, careful and considerate!" A fitting slogan for all sorts of activity, you may agree, but all too often neglected in the corporate violence of everyday modern existence. It is not too surprising if some people are simply not able to leave this disruptive attitude behind them when they knock off work for a couple of weeks. They haven't been educated to behave any better, that's all.

The only real solution to this irritating problem is a concept which comes under the heading of "etiquette". It's a quaint old-fashioned word implying the idea of good behaviour and that you should not do things to others which you would not like them to do to you. To achieve an acceptable standard in this practice is amazingly easy. All you have to do is think before you act.

For instance, when on the water try to behave as if you were going to fish the same stretch again half an hour later. This means disturbing the water and fish as little as possible. The easiest way to achieve this is to keep wading to a minimum so the fish are not frightened any more than is necessary, and to stay as far away from the water as you can when walking along the bank – if you can't see the water then the fish can't see you. Don't throw stones in the water, even if you have an almost overwhelming urge to punish something, anything, after a fruitless, fishless outing. Put discarded nylon, hooks and weights in your pocket and take them home for proper disposal. Do the same with your sandwich and sticky-bun wrappers. In short, treat the water quietly and with respect for the benefit of anyone who may be working their way up behind you.

When two anglers who are going in opposite directions on a river meet each other, convention demands that the one working downstream should stop fishing as soon as the one working up is sighted – or on a big river, is a minimum of 50 yards (45.7 metres) away. It's the same logic as two cars meeting on a steep, narrow hill; the one going down stops to allow the one going up to pass.

If you catch up with another angler moving more slowly in the same direction it is only simple courtesy to stop, not only to compare notes, but to inform the slow mover you will leave a certain length of water undisturbed before starting to fish again. And stick to your word! Don't start flogging the water again as soon as you are out of sight or you will diminish yourself, as well as demonstrating your ability to lie. Such an action is almost as bad as crossing directly in front of another angler and running the risk of tangled lines or multiple contusions.

Some anglers have a habit of starting to fish a pool and remaining in that pool all day. For the disabled, no-one would object, but for others it again shows a lack of consideration. We all know those who selfishly indulge in this practice. Unfortunately, "hogging the water" is all too prevalent on some of the more popular salmon holding pools, so much so that some clubs have had to introduce a regulation to proscribe this conduct. This normally states a time limit, typically twenty minutes or so, after which time the angler fishing the pool has to move on if another angler indicates he wishes to fish in the same place. It usually works quite well because the inclusion of such a rule highlights the need for at least a basic standard of courtesy. With a little luck it will also manifest itself in other ways to cure bad habits and thoughtlessness.

Coarse fishing venues or lakeside angling are in a different category, of course, since they do not involve much movement along the bank, or "roaming". Still, on heavily fished waters, it is always a mark of consideration to position yourself far enough away from other anglers to preclude the chance of entanglement with your nearest neighbour's tackle. Simple good manners, this.

As far as the differences between varying disciplines of angling are concerned, the only convention observed by a courteous fisherman is that the spinner will always give way to any other form of fishing. The reason for this is that spinning is a much faster way of covering the water and consequently the angler using a spinner travels more rapidly along the river. Thus it is not asking too much to expect him to miss a bit – all else being equal, of course.

In this tiny roadside brook, during mid-December, the author watched a heron capture a half-pound trout up for spawning from the lake a quarter of a mile away.

Even the most prolific of waters usually have a bag limit imposed by the local club. That's how they remain prolific. Imagine the situation if there were a free-for-all as it used to be! It wouldn't be long before fish life virtually disappeared with only the tiddlers left – and not many of them, either. It has happened on many popular waters in the past.

If your ticket specifies a catch or size limit, stick to it, if only for the reason that your bag may be inspected by a bailiff or any other person empowered to do so. Transgression may, at the very least, result in your being asked to leave the water forthwith and never return. Quite right, too! If no catch or size limit is specified, impose your own and never remove more fish from the water than you require for a tasty meal. Only immature anglers feel the need continually to prove themselves in this way. Despise or pity them as your nature dictates. And no taking the limit back to the car then returning to the river for another lot, either!

A sensible, self-imposed limit would be no more than three decent-sized fish. This is all the author ever takes home if he is lucky enough to catch as much as this and he makes sure anyone who accompanies him on a fishing trip adheres to the same ethic. Those who don't are only given one more chance to develop a sense of responsibility and water-care before they cease to be invited. On tiny streams, of course, the fish may not grow big enough to be worth eating. Just return them all, then! That way they'll still be around to provide a good day's sport next time you decide to pay them a visit.

Mention is made above of the bailiff and others empowered to inspect your catch, but how do you know who is a bailiff or another member of the angling club and who isn't? Bearing in mind the old adage that attack is the best form of defence, it is not unknown for an angler who is not entitled to fish the water to pose as a bailiff and demand the production of your permit. To eliminate the possibility of a poacher laughing at you behind your back, always ask for his authorization. This will either be an ID card in the case of a River Authority bailiff or a current club membership. If these cannot be produced you have the choice of ignoring him, asking him to go away (or words to that effect), or instructing him to leave the water immediately.

Care of the landowner's property is vitally important. Even if his riverside fields are full of rusty old cars, farm machinery or brightly coloured fertiliser and animal feed bags, act as if the surroundings were a perfectly manicured parkland and behave accordingly. Always observe the Countryside Code. If you don't know it, learn it!

Only climb over field gates if they are incapable of being opened, taking care not to damage the hinges and latches. Open them and walk through properly, ensuring they are securely closed behind you unless they were open to begin with. Never park your car in the roadside slot which gives access to a field gate; the farmer will not be very amused if he needs to get his cattle or sheep in or out of that particular field and may be annoyed enough to rent his bit of river to a private individual the following year. The club could lose the water in extreme cases. It has happened many times.

Try very hard not to damage fences or posts when crossing over them. If you can't get over easily look for another crossing point. Avoid creating stress to farm animals especially when they are carrying or nursing young. A nervous, highly-strung pedigree cow can get very upset at being forced to chase you away from its offspring. Frantically legging it over a rough meadow won't do *you* much good either. For this reason, among others, it is not recommended that dogs accompany you on the river. Even the best-behaved Fido can upset a timid sheep or cow. A prudent farmer will use a shotgun first and enquire about the ownership of a potentially ferocious dog afterwards.

Then there is the water itself! A little trimming of riverside foliage will rarely be frowned upon as long as whole rows of trees are not felled indiscriminately. The removal of a branch which restricts a cast into a pool or run is beneficial to all who come after. Cutting to retrieve tangled and possibly expensive end-tackle is a necessity. Wholesale demolition of foliage can be counter-productive as every river needs the occasional inaccessible pool to maintain a resident head of fish. Left undisturbed, such pools can provide a welcome challenge on an otherwise bland stretch, as well as providing a much needed refuge for larger specimens, the capture of which can be considered to be a real achievement. Fishing which is too easy can sometimes be pretty boring, too.

Bearing these points in mind, a considerate angler will always attempt to improve the quality of the water while he is fishing – it is as much to his own benefit as for others. Try to do something, no matter how small, each time you go to the river. We have all seen supermarket trolleys lying on the bottom of a pool, plastic bags trapped among waterside branches, and other litter fouling the banks. Like they say about the poor: antisocial pigs are always among us. This is to be found all over Britain, a natural consequence of an affluent society, some may say. The wealthier the pigs, the more they have to discard.

Nobody who cares for their surroundings will accept this and it is up to the anglers using the water to do something about it. There is no need to drag a builder's skip along with you but you can at least remove the larger offending articles from the water. An old mattress, for instance, that some slob has thrown from a bridge can completely ruin a pool by its very presence. Pull it out if you can. Lug it to a convenient position and contact the local authority rubbish disposal depot the next day and ask them to collect it when one of their lorries next passes the location. Even better if you can accumulate a nice big pile of junk to make their trip more worthwhile.

The river you may choose to fish on your holiday may have very little in the way of rubbish scattered about. Indeed, most Welsh rivers are well-kept, some clubs being very keen to keep their water that way and organising regular cleaning and trimming expeditions to ensure its continued quality. The trick is to stop the litter-louts in the first place.

This is where *you* can help, both on your holiday water, back on your home patch, or anywhere else you go.

Keep your eyes open at bridges, lay-bys and at places where the road runs alongside a river. You are looking for two things; lorries apparently rearranging or transferring their cargo, and cars either towing a trailer or simply parked, with someone standing idly by, seemingly waiting for you to get out of sight. You often get a sort of *feeling* about these things. An air of furtiveness is often observed. The other thing to watch for is a tanker lorry with its hosepipe down a roadside drain or over the hedge.

Lorries rearranging or transferring cargo will nearly always find a lot of packaging which has to be disposed of. Responsible drivers (the vast majority) will stow it away for proper processing when they return to the depot. Others (the small minority) will simply leave it at the roadside or throw it over a hedge. If you see this practice, make a note of the time (this can be very important in these days of tachographs) and at least get the company name from the side of the lorry and/or a registration number. Then make a complaint to the company. Depending on their attitude, a further complaint may have to be made to the local authority or police. A photograph can be extremely useful in obtaining a successful prosecution.

Local authority cleansing departments have lorries which clean out roadside drains. These tankers will have the emblem of the department prominently displayed somewhere on the bodywork. Tankers other than these with a hosepipe down a drain or over a hedge must always be viewed with suspicion because disposing of a load of sludge or poisonous liquid is much more profitable if fees for the use of authorised sites can be avoided.

A whole tankerful of waste oil, at least 1.000 gallons of it (4,545 litres), was poured down a road drain at a local river bridge a couple of years ago. Plenty of people remembered seeing the lorry but no-one thought to obtain any information which indicated ownership. It's not easy to see whether a drain is being cleaned out or used as a dump. Thousands of fish died and the river still has not properly recovered.

Once again, note the time, try to get a company name, registration number and a photo if possible then go downstream with a few clean containers and obtain three water samples at ten minute intervals before phoning the river authority. If you only have a single container, wait until any pollution is evident before taking your sample. In fact, it is a good idea always to carry a small, clean bottle with you when going fishing. Any pollution seen entering the river, whether it is from an industrial source or farm slurry, should be reported immediately to the river authority and a sample collected for evidence.

An excellent section of Llyn Clywedog (615 acres) set in the magnificent scenery of mid-Wales. Brown and rainbow trout are big and plentiful, access is good and facilities are first class. Very suitable for disabled anglers.

The third type of dumping, that of disposing of household rubbish in the countryside or river, is more reprehensible. Surely it would not be much further to go to a proper disposal amenity. These authorised sites are free, after all!

People who indulge in this practice must be dealt with severely, so if you ever see anyone actually dumping, get the registration number and a photo if possible. If you suspect that they may only be waiting until there is no-one around, stop within sight until they move on. The trouble with this is they will only go somewhere else, or come back again later. Some people will go to great lengths to mess things up for others.

Lastly, poaching. Everyone knows that the old-time poacher who took an occasional fish for the table is an endangered species.

He has been replaced by the organized gang capable of wiping out whole stretches of river and whose sole motive is to make plenty of profit by selling the catch. They will use nets, diving gear and spears, poison, and anything else they can think of.

If you ever see such an operation in progress, walk away! The only thing you can safely do is search for the vehicle they came in, make a note of the registration number and the time, then contact the river authority immediately on their freephone number. With a bit of luck the perpetrators will be caught in the act and prosecuted by both the river authority and the angling club. Confiscation of equipment, including vehicles used, is mandatory.

The other kind of poacher who dons bathing trunks on a hot day and gropes around under the stones can be just as detrimental to the fishing. Leaving aside the disturbance they cause to the water you have paid to fish, some of them just don't know when to stop and can fill a couple of plastic shopping bags with fish in a day. These folk must be ordered to leave the river immediately unless you wish to have the fishery ruined.

Wales is a beautiful place, extremely beautiful, as well as having a big slice of the best fishing in Britain. We, as anglers with the best interests of our rivers at heart, want to keep it that way. Anyone who acts in a contrary manner should expect to be dealt with as harshly as the law allows. They must be taught the meaning of courtesy, care and consideration. In short – etiquette! Please assist the natives to keep Wales beautiful and prolific, not only for the sake of future generations but for your next holiday as well.

Don't allow the spoilers to win!

Appendix 1

Major Club Waters

Here is a quick-reference list of Welsh rivers on which there is at least one club holding a substantial stretch AT THE PRESENT TIME. It must be remembered that not all clubs will hold the freehold to their fishing; some have a lot (or even all) their rights on a leasehold or annual rental basis and these have been known to disband and disappear from the scene if sufficient leases are not renewed for any reason.

You will have to refer to your specialist "Where to fish" book for more detailed information about the location of the waters on which you can purchase a ticket.

The list commences in the north-east corner of Wales with the Dee and continues anticlockwise, ending back on the English border with the upper Severn.

Type of fish awaiting your pursuit:-

- S: Salmon
- ST: Sea-trout (*Sewin*)
- T: Brown Trout
- C: Coarse Fish

DEE *(DYFRDWY)* Many club and private holdings where tickets are available, right up to near the source above Bala Lake (*Llyn Tegid*). S, T, C.

CLWYD A few short holdings in the lower reaches. Most of the rest in hotel or other private hands. S, ST, T.

CONWAY *(CONWY)* Clubs at Dolgarrog, Llanrwst and Betws-y-coed. The rest in private hands, some of which will issue permits. S, ST, T.

OGWEN One main club with lots of water including other rivers and lakes. S, ST, T.

SEIONT *(SAINT)* Most of this river is under the control of one major club which also has holdings on the Gwyrfai and the Llyfni as well as on several lakes including Padarn, Cwellyn, Dywarchen and Llyn-y-gadair. S, ST, T. (Arctic char in Llyn Padarn).

ERCH & RHYD-HIR Ample ticket water on these two small but delightful rivers close to Pwllheli. S, ST, T.

DWYFOR Many stretches controlled by the local club based at Cricieth. S, ST, T.

GLASLYN Miles of club water ranging from deep canal-like stretches in the lower reaches to a mountain torrent near Beddgelert. S, ST, T.

DWYRYD A club based at Blaenau Ffestiniog offers water to suit all game angling tastes from a wide river, through plunging gorges and right up to the mountain tops as well as a selection of lakes. S, ST, T.

MAWDDACH The major expanse of club water is on the Wnion, a major tributary running through Dolgellau, but a lot of ticket water is also available on the main river and the Eden tributary. S, ST, T.

DYSYNNI Middle and upper reaches available on this small but prolific (for sea-trout later in the season) river. S, ST, T.

DOVEY (DYFI) The deserved fame of this legendary sea-trout river has made it necessary for a highly restrictive policy to be imposed by the club controlling most of the best water. Arrange your permit well in advance to avoid disappointment. S, ST, T.

RHEIDOL & YSTWYTH Many miles of river and very many lakes controlled by the major club on these waters. S, ST, T.

AERON Several miles of ticket water available on this sometimes difficult but rewarding river. S, ST, T.

NEVERN (NYFER) A small river but with sufficient club water for a holiday in the vicinity. S, ST, T.

TEIFI Plenty of ticket water throughout this long river. The three major clubs with extensive holdings are based at Newcastle Emlyn, Llandysul and Tregaron. A lot of private ticket water to be had if you know where to look. S, ST, T.

CLEDDAU A very long stretch is managed on the western Cleddau by a club based in Haverfordwest. S, ST, T.

TOWY *(TYWI)* The clubs at Carmarthen have a lot of water on the Towy and several other rivers in the vicinity. Club permits can also be obtained for stretches at Llandeilo, Llangadog and Llandovery with other smaller ticket beats scattered here and there. S, ST, T.

LOUGHOR *(LLWCHWR)* There are several clubs sharing the bounty of this short, varied river. S, ST, T.

TAWE Nearly all of this underrated river is controlled by just two clubs whose waters meet at Pontardawe. Excellent fishing, half of it in semi-urban surroundings with coarse fish in the last few kilometres to the sea. S, ST, T, C.

NEATH *(NEDD)* Another much underrated river, attracting heavy runs of migratory fish. Two main clubs to choose from. S, ST, T.

ELY *(ELAI)*, RHONDDA, TAFF *(TAF)*, EBBW *(EBWY)* & RHYMNEY *(RHYMNI)* These rocky trout-filled waters in urban surroundings within the old coal-mining valleys are well served by many clubs which issue tickets to visitors. Some clubs also have good coarse fishing to offer. T, C.

USK *(WYSG)* Mostly in private hands, unfortunately, although there are clubs with reasonable stretches at Crickhowell, Usk and Brecon. Other clubs, some from outside the immediate area, hold water on which tickets can be obtained. There are a few other private stretches run by hotels and farms which will issue a day ticket. S, T, C.

WYE *(GWY)* What can be said about the Wye that hasn't been said before? Everyone knows it's a wonderful river. Trouble is, like the Usk, it's mostly private. The main clubs are centred at Ross, Hereford, Builth Wells and Rhayader. Other private and hotel water is available throughout the course of the river. S, T, C.

SEVERN *(HAFREN)* Only the upper-middle reaches and headwaters are within the Welsh border to the west of Crew Green. Many of the tributaries like the Vyrnwy, Tanat and Rhiw have riverside hotels and farms where tickets can be obtained. The three main clubs are the Birmingham AA, the club at Llanidloes and the Montgomery AA which has extensive waters (river, lake and canal) throughout the whole watershed. S, T, C.

Appendix 2

Coarse and Sea Fishing Information

Here is a list of venues where Welsh coarse fish are to be found. The lake names are followed by the name of the nearest town. For information on where to obtain a permit either consult your "Where to fish" book or make local enquiries.

RIVERS

DEE Many species including grayling throughout the whole of the river.

CEFNI (Anglesey) The only coarse fishing river in Anglesey but fish are small and not in great numbers.

TAWE (nr. Swansea) From Morriston downstream to the Barrage – about 4/5 miles. A few species present, including chub, and the situation is constantly improving. This will almost certainly become an important coarse fishery in the near future.

USK Crickhowell downstream. Several species with roach and dace as the most common.

WYE Coarse fish in abundance all the way up to Rhayader and in all major tributaries. Grayling, chub, pike – you name it!

SEVERN The main river and major tributaries harbour chub, grayling, dace, roach, pike, etc. All our old favourites including, it is whispered, a chance at a barbel.

CANALS

SHROPSHIRE UNION Plenty of choice in species and venues from Chester all the way up to where it spills from the River Severn near Newtown and including the Llangollen Spur.

NEATH VALLEY Two canals to choose from here, one each side of the valley. Pike, tench and carp provide the big 'uns while perch, roach and rudd fill the gaps.

MONMOUTHSHIRE AND BRECON CANAL Great variety and plenty of them.

LAKES

On a few of these coarse fishing waters the prospects of obtaining a permit to fish can be somewhat ambiguous. It is recommended that local enquiries are made if your "Where to fish" book does not mention them.

WEPRE POOL, Connah's Quay, Clwyd.
TRAP POOL, Buckley, Clwyd.

FLASH LAKE, Gresford.
ACTON PARK LAKE, Wrexham.
BALA LAKE, Bala, Gwynedd.
LLYN CORON, Aberffraw.
LLYN MAELOG, Rhosneigr, Anglesey.
LLYN CERRIG BACH, Rhosneigr. Anglesey.
LLYN DINAM, Holyhead, Anglesey.
LLYN TŴR, Holyhead, Anglesey.
CEFNI RESERVOIR, Llangefni, Anglesey.
LLYN BODAFON, Llanallgo, Anglesey.
TRAWSFYNYDD LAKE, Trawsfynydd, Gwynedd.
HAFOD-Y-LLYN, nr. Llanbedr, south Gwynedd.
TALLEY LAKES, Talley, Llandeilo, Dyfed.
BOSHERTON LAKES, Pembroke, Dyfed.
BISHOP'S POOL, Carmarthen, Dyfed.
FAIRWOOD LODGE LAKE, Upper Killay, Swansea.
SWANSEA ENTERPRISE ZONE PONDS, Morriston, Swansea.
BENDLE'S POND, Skewen, Neath.
SQUARE POND, Briton Ferry, Neath.
KENFIG POOL, Pyle, nr. Porth-cawl.
PWLL-Y-WAUN POND, Porth-cawl.
WILDERNESS POND, Porth-cawl.
DARREN LAKE, Ferndale, nr. Pontypridd.
WEBBER'S POND, Merthyr Tydfil.
NANT MOEL CYNON, Hirwaun, nr. Aberdare.
NANT-HIR RESERVOIR, Hirwaun, nr. Aberdare.
RHOS-LAS RESERVOIR, Rhymney.
FOCHRHIW POND, Blackwood, Gwent.
SANDS POND, Bedlinog.

BRYN-CAE-OWEN POND, Merthyr Tydfil.
CYFARTHFA LAKE, Merthyr Tydfil.
PONTSTICILL RESERVOIR, Merthyr Tydfil.
ROATH PARK LAKE, Cardiff.
CAERFFILI LAKE, Caerffili, nr. Cardiff.
CEFN GOLAU POND, Tredegar.
BUTETOWN RESERVOIR, Rhymney.
PEN-Y-WERN PONDS, Merthyr Tydfil.
LISWERRY POND, Newport, Gwent.
TREDEGAR HOUSE LAKE, Newport, Gwent.
WOODSTOCK POND, Newport, Gwent.
CWMBRÂN LAKE, Cwmbrân, nr. Newport, Gwent.
BOAT POND (and several others), Ebbw Vale.
LLANGORSE LAKE *(LLYN SYFADDAN)*, Llan-gors, nr. Brecon.
PYSGODLYN FARM POND, Cradoc, nr. Brecon.
DDERW POOLS, Llys-wen, nr. Brecon.
WEST END FARM LAKE, Docklow, nr. Leominster.
MILTON POOL, Pembridge, nr. Kington.
FLINTSHAM POOL, Titley, nr. Kington.
LLANDRINDOD LAKE, Llandrindod Wells, Powys.

Quite a lot, eh? Bet you didn't realize how many there are in Wales – and these are only the ones of which the author has personal knowledge; there may well be many others. Nobody's perfect! It is certain that many trout farms have pools set aside for the convenience of coarse fishermen. Wales can cater very well for this branch of the sport.

Live bait can be very hard to obtain in some areas if you don't know where to look for it. To assist the sea angler, there follows a rough guide to beaches where lugworms, ragworms, razor fish and sand eels may be found. Soft crab and small fish can be found in the pools and under weed on any rocky shore, of course. Once more we shall start in the north-east and work anticlockwise.

Along the continuous sandy strand from Point of Ayr to Rhos-on-Sea patchy lug can be found; often hard digging until you get to know where the best bits are. On the nightmare rocky beach west of Rhos-on-Sea there is a chance of finding a few king rag, but don't hold your breath!

The next place for lug is in the Conway estuary on both the Deganwy and Conway town shores. Plenty of harbour rag in the muddy bits and a fair sprinkling of albino rag – ideal for mixing with cockles for a cocktail. For use as bait, of course!

Bait then becomes rather rare until you get to Bangor Pier and the Penrhyn Port area. Nice and muddy here. Small ragworm in abundance.

The island of Anglesey has many beaches where lugworm can be obtained. Try Red Wharf Bay, the tidal reaches each side of the Stanley Embankment carrying the A5 close to Holyhead, the coves around Rhosneigr (hard going here), Aberffraw Bay and Malltraeth Sands.

South of Caernarfon on the mainland is Foryd Bay. Plenty of nice lugworms here.

The Lleyn Peninsula is noted for its shortage of worm-type baits. A few lugworms may be found in the harbour at Trefor, on Nefyn beaches, and in the western bit of Aberdaron beach. From here on the situation improves a bit, getting better as you travel east. There are a few razor fish at low tide in Hell's Mouth Bay (aptly named when a south-westerly gale is up), but the next decent places for lugworms are in Aber-soch and Pwllheli harbours and on Aber-soch beach to the south of the town.

Lugworms also maintain an extensive ghetto below the embankment at Portmadoc. Proceeding south, the next worthwhile location is in the estuary of the River Artro at Llanbedr. Ragworms swarm in the smelly harbour mud at Barmouth and there is an even chance of razor fish out on the sands in front of the town – but it's a long walk! Just over the river at Fairbourne there are some lugworms but digging them can be a risky business owing to fierce currents and an unstable watercourse. Best to start as soon as the tide has retreated enough and leave well before it starts to come in.

The sands within the Dovey estuary at Ynys-las provide lugworms – reluctantly – but from here southwards they are almost impossible to find until you reach New Quay. The next place is on Poppitt sands at Cardigan. Here there are plenty. Fishguard harbour has some too, along with small ragworms. So does Solva Harbour.

As far as the banks of the haven around Milford are concerned, there are plenty of small ragworms and occasional patches of lug among the mud but the best lugworms are to be found along the eastern shore in Angle bay. Even a few razor fish here and in Broadhaven. Razor fish and a few lug can also be found west of Saundersfoot harbour, but this can be a very busy place in summer time.

Lots of lugworm and a few razors on Pendine beach. A long walk is necessary to get to the best beds. Rag, lug and cockles are in plenty all round the Towy estuary. Only take away the occasional cockle dug up in pursuit of worms from the commercial cockle beds! Better still, leave them alone and purchase them locally because some of the locals gather them for a living. The town beaches at Llanelli are good for lug, so is Salthouse point over the water at Crofty near Pen-clawdd. The cockle beds on this (south) side of the Loughor estuary are famed world-wide and the local economy is dependant upon their harvesting. Please don't go digging in the cockle beds! Ragworms infest the mud all over this estuary.

The Gower Peninsula has a shortage of bait, most of the local anglers preferring to get their supplies in Swansea Bay. Plenty of smallish lugworms in the west of this bay and they get bigger and juicier as you go east – and scarcer.

East of here, wherever there is mud, you can find ragworms. Lug patches are rather far apart but where they are found there tends to be a lot of them. Big black ones too! Depending on where you are staying, you can try the east side of Trecco Bay at Porth-cawl, the mouth of the River Ogmore, Watchtower Bay, Barry, the foreshore at Cardiff Docks, either side of the mouth of the Usk at Newport and at various points east.

Appendix 3

Facilities for the Disabled Angler

There are many differing types of disability ranging from giddiness to impaired vision or mobility to severe mobility problems requiring confinement to a wheelchair. For the latter, locomotion along the average river bank is out of the question due to the unevenness of fields and pathways. Getting close enough to the water to do any fishing is even more difficult; pebbly shores or rocky cliffs do not lend themselves to those unable to walk independently, although there are a few associations who have invested in a hard standing with vehicular access and more are planned for the near future. Generally speaking these have been quite successful due to careful thought about their locations. Catches by handicapped fishermen have often exceeded those of the fully mobile.

The situation is even better on some stillwaters where, as long as a motor vehicle can get close enough to the waterside, the opportunities for the severely disabled to catch their fair share of fish are generally excellent. Coarse fishermen are fairly well served in this respect, so are those who wish to tempt trout in the Welsh reservoirs - many of which provide adequate facilities for disabled anglers.

The Tawe at Glais. Clive, holding the rod, plays out a 7lb salmon the day after the new disabled fishing pitch was opened for business.

Rivers are a different matter. They are also all different in the manner of obstacle they can place in the path of a partially disabled person. This appendix is mostly for the benefit of those who are able to get around without the use of a wheelchair yet limited in the type of water they can fish owing to troubles with their lower limbs, respiratory or cardiac problems, and general infirmity due to an advanced age.

Mention has been made in Chapter 8 of the lack of thought by some angling clubs as regards the welfare of partially disabled anglers where access to the water is concerned. Resisting the urge to flog this particular issue to death, any partially disabled angler who has no idea of the character of the river he wishes to fish on his Welsh holiday could well be in for a shock unless he is prepared to take a risk. He could well find most of the water is effectively beyond his reach by virtue of the rugged terrain he may have to negotiate.

The following is a list of Welsh rivers giving their accessibility ratings for the partially disabled along with a few brief observations for further guidance. The accessible stretches may not necessarily match with those under the control of a club which issues tickets. You can ascertain that fact by phoning the number of the nearest permit distributor listed in your "Where to fish" book.

RATINGS

*** Generally good access to water, relatively gentle banks and/or ample safe, shallow wading.

** Generally fair. Rockier than above, access to the water sometimes difficult and crossing of the river sometimes necessary.

* Difficult and potentially dangerous. Deep gorges. Hard to get on to the river bank more often than not, and lots of big, slippery boulders or dangerous smooth-rock pools and banks.

These ratings are based upon the assumed ability of a person with middle-range respiratory, cardiac (e.g. angina) or lower limb problems (e.g. prosthetic leg or unstable footing). Also relevant for the elderly and young children. It must be remembered that due to the varied nature of most Welsh rivers throughout their courses, there will be certain stretches within the generalized sections which are more (or less) difficult than indicated below. There are always exceptions to the general rule. This list is merely a loose guide to bank and wading safety and should not be assumed to bear any relationship to the quality or availability of the fishing.

PART OF RIVER

L: Lower reaches
M: Middle reaches
U: Upper reaches

River	L	M	U	Advice Notes
Dee (*Dyfrdwy*)	***	**	**	
Clwyd	***	**	**	
Conway (*Conwy*)	***	*	**	M: Be cautious above Betws-y-Coed. The Fairy Glen, for instance, is highly dangerous.
Ogwen	*	*	**	L&M: Certain parts can be rather hazardous.
Seiont (*Saint*)	**	**	**	Violent in spate. Wade carefully!
Gwyrfai	*	***	**	
Llyfni	*	*	***	M: A few sections can be dangerous in the middle reaches.

River				Notes
Dwyfor	**	**	***	
Glaslyn	***	*	**	
Dwyryd	***	***	*	Some very hazardous gorges.
Artro	*	*	***	L&M: Difficult river bed for wading. This can be an extremely violent river in spate.
Wnion	***	*	**	
Mawddach	***	*	*	
Dysynni	***	**	***	
Dovey (*Dyfi*)	***	***	*	The Twymyn and Dugoed gorges are DANGEROUS most of their length. Be very careful here!
Rheidol	***	***	*	
Ystwyth	***	**	*	
Aeron	**	**	**	
Teify (*Teifi*)	**	***	***	
Cleddau	**	**	**	
Taf	**	**	**	
Towy (*Tywi*)	***	***	**	
Loughor (Llwchwr)	*	***	**	L: High, muddy banks.
Tawe	***	***	**	
Neath (*Nedd*)	***	***	*	U: Plenty of caves and waterfalls.
Afan	***	***	***	
Ogmore (*Ogwr*)	**	**	**	
Taff	**	**	**	
Usk (*Wysg*)	***	***	***	
Wye (*Gwy*)	***	***	**	L&M: But take care! Deep, powerful river.
Severn (*Hafren*)			***	

A further snippet of information for anglers who are confined to a wheelchair. It can often be as much of a chore to find suitable accommodation as a suitable spot to cast a line. How much easier it would be if both could be at the same location. Well, there are a few hotels which cater for wheelchairs *as well as* providing fishing for severely disabled guests. Hopefully this facility will become more widely available in the not too far distant future. In the meantime, here is a regrettably short list of those particular hotels known to the author at present.

Aber-nant Lake Hotel, Llanwrtyd Wells, Powys, LD5 4RR.
Tel: 01591 610250. *A fair-sized lake stocked with trout and several species of coarse fish. Fishing free to guests.*

Caer Beris Manor, Garth Rd, Builth Wells, Powys, LD2 3NP.
Tel: 01982 552601. *Big put and take trout in Llyn Alarch.*

Hand Hotel, Llanfair Dyffryn Ceiriog, Nr Llangollen, Clwyd, LL20 7LD. Tel: 01691 600666. *This hotel has no fishing of its own but is always pleased to arrange suitable local venues for the disabled.*

Lake Country House Hotel, Llangamarch Wells, Powys, LD4 4BS.
Tel: 01591 620202.
Large trout in a 3 acre lake. Gillie and boat available if required.

Ty'n-y-cornel Hotel, Tal-y-llyn, Tywyn, Gwynedd, LL36 9A. Tel: 01654 782282. *Large well-stocked trout lake with boats. Some assistance may be needed with the accommodation.*

Appendix 4

Welsh Accommodation with Fishing

A list of some of the best-known hotels offering fishing in their tariffs is reproduced here in alphabetical order of rivers, and it is not all-encompassing. The majority are able to supply packed meals for extended fishing sessions and some will cater for night fishing by arrangement and accommodate dogs. A lot of them - not all - offer permits to non-residents; it is always best to phone in advance to enquire about this if it matters to you. There are several others - those below just happen to be known to the author from personal experience. Unless otherwise stated the fishing is an extra charge on accommodation.

CLWYD Ruthin Castle Hotel, Ruthin. This impressive hostelry allows free fishing for guests on many of the best stretches on the beautiful river Clwyd with some smaller stream fishing as well. Salmon, sea-trout and browns are in abundance.

CONWAY (*Conwy*) Gwydyr Hotel, Betws-y-coed. A famous name in the annals of game fishing; 8 miles (13 km) of first class salmon and sea-trout water on three rivers. Also miles of river and lake fishing for brownies. Mini breaks available.

DEE *(Dyfrdwy)* Bryn Howel Hotel and Restaurant, Llangollen. Five miles superlative fishing for salmon, trout and grayling (among others). Free to guests.

DOVEY (*Dyfi*) Brigands Inn, Mallwyd; 3 miles (5 km) upper middle reaches. Salmon, sea-trout and lakes holding brownies and rainbows. Night fishing catered for.

ELAN VALLEY Elan Valley Hotel, Rhayader; 1,600 acres (657 hectares) of reservoirs with further access to 5 miles (8 km) of the Wye, 3 miles (4.82 km) on the Marteg and a fine put and take lake.

IRFON Aber-nant Lake Hotel, Llawrtyd Wells; 1.25 miles left bank and a lake stocked with trout and coarse fish free to guests.

IRFON Camarch Hotel, Llangamarch Wells. Can provide fishing on the Irfon, Dulais, Camarch and Wye. Add grayling to the usual list of things to catch.

IRFON Lake House Country Hotel, Llangamarch Wells. About 2.5 miles (4 km) of river and a 3 acre (1.21 hectares) lake. The Irfon is a very good grayling river.

ITHON Severn Arms Hotel, Pen-y-bont, nr. Llandrindod Wells; 6 miles excellent trout and grayling fishing free to guests. Several coarse species including some big chub.

LAKE VYRNWY Lake Vyrnwy Hotel. In a beautiful location on the shores of this famous reservoir. 1100 acres (445 hectares) regularly stocked with browns and rainbows. Luxurious accommodation. Boats available.

MAWDDACH Dolmelynllyn Hall Hotel, Ganllwyd, Dolgellau. Many miles of angling for trout and migratory fish on the Wnion, a major tributary, as well as the main river. Fishing free to guests. This is a non-smoking establishment with a fine reputation for its cuisine.

MAWDDACH Ty'n-y-groes Hotel, Ganllwyd, Dolgellau. An excellent stretch directly opposite this small, cosy hostelry with easy access. A 17lb (7.711 kg) sea-trout recently succumbed to the efforts of one of the guests.

SEVERN *(Hafren)* Lion Hotel, Llandinam, nr. Newtown. Nearly four miles double bank of first-class grayling water with trout as back-up.

TAL-Y-LLYN LAKE Ty'n-y-cornel Hotel. Superb setting alongside the second highest mountain in Wales. Its 220 acres (89 hectares) are regularly stocked with brown trout. Migratory fish enter this lake in the latter part of the season. Boats available. Also on offer is a 45 acre (18.21 hectares) high mountain lake at 1,700 ft (518 meters) and four and a half miles (7.24 km) of migratory fish water on the river Dysynni.

TEIFI Castell Malgwyn Hotel, Llechryd, Cardigan. Two and a quarter miles (3.62 km) left bank of the lower reaches of the Teifi holding salmon, sea trout and some big brownies. Definitely worth a visit. Free to guests.

USK (*Wysg*) Gliffaes Hotel, Crickhowell. Way out in the country. Controls a mile and three quarters (2.82 km) on two stretches. Salmon and a lot of really hefty river brownies. First class for dry fly in low water.

USK (*Wysg*) Usk Hotel, Tal-y-bont on Usk. One mile (1.61 km) left bank. Well worth a stay for very rewarding trout fishing with the occasional salmon.

USK *(Wysg)* Pen-pont, west of Brecon. Bed and breakfast accommodation. Over a mile both banks. Extremely good fly water holding plenty of large trout. Salmon later in season.

WYE *(Gwy)* Caer Beris Manor, Builth Wells. Over half a mile on the Irfon free to guests and a further 4 miles on the Wye and Irfon.

The hotels listed above are those which control the larger stretches of rivers or lakes. There are quite a few others which not only have smaller stretches, sometimes on small streams, but are also close to club waters on which a ticket may be obtained. These are well worth investigating if only because their own waters can be used at any time without having to travel far; an ideal situation if you do not intend to fish all day, every day. Please do not assume that the quality of the fishing is in any way inferior to that listed above, most of it is excellent. Much of it is free: the list below indicates where this applies. The free fishing only applies for those actually staying at the hotel, of course. A list of those which have been known to the author is as follows.

River	Hotel	
Alwen	Crown Hotel, Llanfihangel Glyn Myfyr	Free
Alwen	Royal Oak Hotel, Glyn Ceiriog, nr. Llangollen	Free
Cain	Bodfach Hall Hotel, Llanfyllin	Free
Ceiriog	Royal Oak Hotel, Glyn Ceiriog	Free
Ceiriog	West Arms Hotel, Llanarmon Dyffryn Ceiriog	Free
Cothi	Glanyrannell Park Hotel, Crug-y-bar, nr. Llandeilo.	
Cothi	Forest Arms Hotel, Brechfa.	
Cothi	Cothi Bridge Hotel, Nantgaredig, nr. Carmarthen.	Free
Cothi	Dolaucothi Arms, Pumsaint.	
Conway	Mount Garmon Hotel, Betws-y-coed.	
Dee	Hand Hotel, Llangollen.	Free
Dee	Owain Glyn Dŵr Hotel, Corwen.	Free
Dovey	Dolbrodmaeth Inn, Dinas Mawddwy.	Free
Lledr	Castell Elen Hotel, Dolwyddelan.	Free
Llyn Cwellyn	Castell Cidwm Hotel, Betws Garmon.	Free
Severn	Maes-mawr Hall Hotel, Caersŵs.	
Summergil	Eagle Hotel, New Radnor, Powys.	Free
Tanat	Horseshoe Inn, Llanyblodwel, nr. Oswestry.	
Teifi	Black Lion Hotel, Llanybydder.	
Teifi	Emlyn Arms Hotel, Newcastle Emlyn	
Usk	Bell Hotel, Glangrwyney, Abergavenny	
Ystwyth	Glyn-wern Guest House, Llanilar.	Free

For further hotel details see the book by the same author to be published in 1997.

Self-Catering Accommodation

For those who prefer to really get away from it all by staying in a cottage or farmhouse on a self-catering basis, there are several agencies to choose from. All will have been inspected and the price will reflect the standard (or status) of property on offer. Many will accept pets and quite a number will have a stretch of fishing often included in the price. A list of agents known to the writer is as follows:

North Wales Holiday Cottages and Farmhouses
Station Road, Deganwy, Conwy, Gwynedd, LL31 9DF.
Tel: 01492 582492

Mann's Holidays
Gaol Street, Pwllheli, Gwynedd, LL53 5DB.
Tel: 01758 613666

Wales Holidays, The Bank, Newtown, Powys.
Tel: 01686 628200

Coastal Cottages of Pembrokeshire
2 Riverside Quay, Haverfordwest, Pembrokeshire, SA61 2LJ.
Tel: 01437 767600

Country Holidays, Spring Mill
Earby, Colne, Lancashire, BB8 6RN.
Tel: 01282 445307

Character Cottages (Holidays) Ltd
34 Fore Street, Sidmouth, Devon, EX10 8AQ.
Tel: 01395 577001

Summer Cottages Ltd
Dorchester, Dorset, DT1 1RE.
Tel: 01305 267545

Ty'n-y-Ffordd; a typical, Welsh, self-catering cottage including three quarters of a mile of the upper Dovey in its rental. Good salmon and sea trout from June on.

Many folk owning self-catering property to let do not use an agent. Most of these tend to take bookings via the outlet of the Welsh Tourist Board. To choose one of these, contact the nearest Tourist Information Office in the area in which you wish to stay.

For a full list of publications, send now for your free
copy of our full-colour, 48-page Catalogue — or just
surf into it on the Internet!

y Lolfa

Talybont
Ceredigion
Cymru
SY24 5HE
e-mail ylolfa@netwales.co.uk
internet http://www.ylolfa.wales.com/
tel. (01970) 832 304
fax 832 782